NEW SELECTED POEMS OF MARYA ZATURENSKA

Portrait of Marya Zaturenska by Francis Criss.

NEW SELECTED POEMS OF

Marya Zaturenska

· · ·

EDITED AND
INTRODUCED BY
Robert Phillips

SYRACUSE UNIVERSITY PRESS

First Edition 2002
02 03 04 05 06 07   6 5 4 3 2 1

The paper used in this publication meets the minimum requirements of
American National Standard for Information Sciences—Permanence of
Paper for Printed Library Materials, ANSI Z39.48–1984.∞™

Library of Congress Cataloging-in-Publication Data
Zaturenska, Marya, 1902–
New selected poems of Marya Zaturenska / edited and introduced by Robert Phillips.—
1st ed.
p. cm.
Includes bibliographical references and index.
ISBN 0-8156-0717-2 (alk. paper)
I. Phillips, Robert S. II. Title.
PS3549.A77 A6 2001
811.52—dc21   2001049510

Manufactured in the United States of America

For Joanna Elizabeth Zeigler and Patrick Bolton Gregory,
and in memory of Horace Gregory

Robert Phillips is Rebecca and John Moores Scholar and professor of English at the University of Houston, where he has taught since 1991. His previous books include six volumes of poetry, three of fiction, and twenty of criticism, belles-lettres, and anthologies. His awards include the Enron Teaching Excellence Award, the Arents Pioneer Medal from Syracuse University, and an Award in Literature from the American Academy of Arts and Letters. He has been a councilor of the Texas Institute of Letters and is poetry editor of the *Texas Review* and chairman of the Poets' Prize.

·   ·   ·

Contents

From *Cold Morning Sky,* 1938

Translations, 1960–1974

· · ·

Introduction

The English critic Cyril Connolly said, "Literary history goes to prove that lyrical poetry is the medium which more than any other defies time." Marya Zaturenska was a consummate lyrical poet. Her work reminds us that the ancient relationship between music and poetry was very much alive in the twentieth century. At a time when the modern and postmodern poets were writing poems as flat as Holland, she gave us the delights of rhymes, rhythms, and the quality of incantation that our forebears valued in poetry.

Born Marya Alexandrovna Zaturensky on September 12, 1902, in Kiev, she was the daughter of Avram Alexander and Johanna (Lupovska) Zaturensky. Her father served in the Russian army during the Russo-Japanese War and was with the Russian forces of occupation in China during the Boxer Uprising. Her mother's family came from Poland and for generations were in the employ of the Prince Radziwell family, living on their estate in a small wooded village. Her mother began work at the age of eight, sewing doll clothes for the Radziwell children. In one interview, the poet recalled being taken to the castle to kiss the hands of the Princess Radziwell, a descendant of Tallyrand. The princess gave Marya her first and only doll. The girl loved Russian and Polish folk songs and made up poems to go with the music before she was old enough to read or write.

The Zaturensky family came to New York City in 1910, when she was eight. They lived on Henry Street, near the Settlement House. Marya was educated in New York public schools, but she had to drop out at age fourteen to help the family make money. (At least she was six years older than her mother had been when she began to work.) She did odd jobs in a factory, but her literary bent eventually delivered her from that drudgery. In her teens, she worked at Brentano's bookshops, and she was a feature writer for a New York newspaper for a year. She also took jobs embroidering; her seamstress mother had taught her how. She worked during the day and attended high school at night.

Since the age of fifteen, Marya had been writing poetry, and she had her first poems published while she was in her teens. In 1920, when she was eighteen, she placed two poems, "A Russian Easter" and "Russian Peasants," with *Poetry: A Magazine of Verse*. Then, as now, it was one of the preeminent poetry journals. She was in the company of Wallace Stevens, Robert Frost, Marianne Moore, James Joyce, and Ezra Pound. The editor, Harriet Monroe, took numerous groups of Zaturenska's poems over the following years. All were published under the name "Marya Zaturensky" until 1931, when the by-line appeared as "Marya Zaturenska." Why she changed the spelling of her surname has never been clear. Perhaps she felt that by 1931 a new start was in order, that she had reached a different stage in her development, and a change in her name represented this shift. Her son, Patrick, suggests another reason: "I assume it was for the sound . . . and because the *a* ending is perhaps the proper feminine one" (1999a). Certainly Zaturenska—for whom the ear was everything—would like the new sound.

A number of her early poems describe the difficulties of tenement life and factory work. She reveals a homesickness for her native Russia, and several show yearnings for release into "Willowsleigh," a City of God, a village known only in her dreams. In one poem, she identified with the Empress Marie Louise, who also longed to return to her ancestral home. Zaturenska couldn't return to Russia, but she found another retreat—the New York Public Library at 42nd Street. Its thick walls became a refuge against the noise and pressure of Manhattan, as well as a free source of thousands of books. It was there that she wrote her earliest poems.

It should be noted that such prodigy was all the more remarkable because she knew no English when she stepped off the boat at Ellis Island. She had no difficulty learning the language; indeed, she said she fell in love with English at first encounter. She told her son that her earliest reading included the novels of John Galsworthy: "She couldn't make much out of what was going on, but she adored the way the characters spoke to each other!" (P. Gregory 1999b). She may also have been attracted to Galsworthy's deep sense of nostalgia and depiction of a departed way of life. Later in life she would expertly translate poems from the Italian and German. How did she learn those languages? They are a joy to read.

In addition to *Poetry,* other journals began to accept her work, including *The Atlantic, The Nation, American Caravan, Herald Tribune Books, The Masses,* and *The Measure.* She began to make literary friends. One was a now-forgotten poet, Edith M. Thomas, who was poetry editor of *Harper's* magazine. She approved of Zaturenska's poems—until she discovered the girl was a regular contributor to Harriet Monroe's *Poetry,* "which she considered the source of all evil," according to Zaturenska. (Founded in 1912, *Poetry* employed Ezra Pound as its first "foreign correspondent," and it was he who coined a motto for the magazine, "To hell with *Harper's* and the magazine touch." Perhaps Miss Thomas had heard the phrase.) Poet Vachel Lindsay became a friend of Zaturenska's, as did John Jay Chapman, a poet, dramatist, and critic. On the other side of the Atlantic, her work caught the attention of English essayist and poet Alice Meynell and poet and novelist Siegfried Sassoon.

She also met an older gentleman named William Webster Ellsworth, a descendent of Noah Webster, the lexicographer known for his *American Dictionary of the English Language* (1828). Ellsworth was a well-known lecturer on literature, and he took an interest in Zaturenska's poetry. He introduced her to his literary circle, which included novelist Willa Cather. At this time, Cather already had published *O Pioneers* and *The Song of the Lark* and would soon win the Pulitzer Prize for *One of Ours.* Meeting Cather changed Zaturenska's life. For it was Cather who got a scholarship for Zaturenska at Valparaiso University in northwestern Indiana. She enrolled in 1922, at the age of twenty, two or three years older than most of her classmates.

Despite her scholarship, Zaturenska was expected to work in addition to her studies, and she found this enervating. The next year, through the graces of her literary friends—Harriet Monroe, Vachel Lindsay, and Willa Cather again—she was sponsored for and awarded a Zona Gale Scholarship at the University of Wisconsin. (Gale was a novelist and playwright, as well as a philanthropist and trustee of the University of Wisconsin. She endowed the Gale Scholarships for writers of promise, of which Zaturenska clearly was one, already having published more poems than many poet-professors.)

Zaturenska transferred to Wisconsin in 1923. She majored in library science, thinking the life of a librarian would allow her the time and quiet to write. The next year, she won the John Reed Memorial Prize from *Poetry* for a group of poems. She worked on the university's literary magazine, which was a distinguished one. Her coeditor was Kenneth Fearing, who went on to be-

come a respected poet and novelist; his novel *The Big Clock* (1946) was made
into a film. The journal's previous coeditors had been poet Horace Gregory
and novelist Margery Latimer. Gregory had graduated from the university the
spring before her enrollment and had moved to New York City, where he
began writing poetry and criticism for the *New Masses,* the *New Republic,* and
the *Nation.* Later he found a job writing real estate advertisements. Even in
his absence, Zaturenska heard much about Horace Gregory, especially from
her advisor, the classicist William Ellery Leonard, translator of Lucretius into
English verse. Leonard spoke highly of Gregory, and Zaturenska was curious
to meet him.

She graduated from the Wisconsin Library School in 1925. She expressed
a desire to continue her studies, this time in history, but funds were lacking.
She concluded her formal education and returned to New York City to live
with her family.

She didn't live with them long. That first summer, her former coeditor,
Fearing, who also was living in New York, introduced her to Horace Gregory.
They immediately fell in love, though Gregory called himself a "predictable
risk" as suitor. During infancy he had contracted tuberculosis of the bone, af-
fecting his spine, which consequently caused paralysis of his left hand and foot
and a tremor in the right hand. He walked with a slight limp. Further, his be-
havior shifted from erratic waves of despair to Micawber-like optimism. Yet
the couple had much in common—the University of Wisconsin, William
Ellery Leonard, Kenneth Fearing, literature, a life of the imagination. He too
had had a group of poems accepted by Harriet Monroe during his last year at
Wisconsin. Gregory was very taken with Zaturenska: "All I saw was a slight,
dark-haired, beautiful girl in a fluttering lilac-tinted organdy dress, who was as
passionately devoted to poetry as I was" (H. Gregory 1971, 163). They mar-
ried that same summer and moved into a dark, one-and-a-half room apart-
ment on the south side of Washington Square. Across the park lived painter
Edward Hopper, whom they would see at the Whitney Museum when its
quarters were on nearby 8th Street. Zaturenska was twenty-three.

A two-week siege of illness cost Gregory his real estate advertising job,
and a period of living by their wits began. It extended into the summer of
1926. Zaturenska was pregnant with their first child, and the couple moved to
three rooms on President Street in Brooklyn. Then Gregory had some luck.
Through a college acquaintance, he was hired as a production man in the
book publishing division of a firm in lower Manhattan that also published

trade journals. This job was short-lived, however, as was another writing for *Women's Wear Daily*. There now were three Gregorys—daughter Joanna had been born, named (more or less) after Zaturenska's mother Johanna. In 1927, the family moved to Sunnyside, a housing development on the outskirts of Long Island City for families in low-income brackets. Gregory continued to try to piece together an income reviewing books. He also swallowed his pride and accepted twenty-five dollars a week from his family back in Wisconsin. Zaturenska's own father was out of work.

A word should be said about Horace Gregory's family. Their circumstances—social, educational, and financial—were in marked contrast to the Zaturenskys. They were Milwaukee aristocracy of Anglo-Irish-Dublin-London origins. His paternal grandfather, Dr. John Gregory, was an astronomer and mathematician at Trinity College, Dublin. He authored several textbooks and is said to have designed the bridges of Phoenix Park, Dublin. After immigrating to southwestern Wisconsin, he became the first city surveyor of Milwaukee and laid out the young urban sprawl. He later was a founder of the University of Wisconsin. His wife was among the first translators of Turgenev from current French translations into English.

His paternal grandmother was the daughter of Henry Goadby, who worked with Darwin, Huxley, Owen, and Tyndall in the early 1860s. Later, he accepted the Chair of Sciences in the newly founded University of Michigan. An uncle edited the *Evening Wisconsin* for twenty years. Gregory's father, Henry Bolton Gregory, was president of a successful firm dispensing bakers' supplies and machinery. At fourteen, he had mastered the Latin texts in the family library inherited from Dr. John Gregory. As an adult, he preferred reading Smollett to the fashionable Tennyson. Gregory himself was given the name Horace Victor Gregory because an aunt thought it was "a fine Latinate name." He was educated at a private school, the German-English Academy, and attended the Milwaukee School of Fine Arts in summers before attending the University of Wisconsin (biographical details from H. Gregory 1956 and 1971).

Given such a privileged background, it is to Gregory's credit that he turned his back on the family fortune. Later, in a bad time, he accepted the weekly "allowance" of twenty-five dollars from his parents. One hundred dollars a month, then, was considerably more than it is today.

Among the Horace Gregorys' new literary friends were the Lewis Mumfords, who lived down the street in Sunnyside, Van Wyck Brooks, Muriel

Rukeyser, James T. Farrell, the Kenneth Burkes, and Malcolm Cowley, then literary editor of the *New Republic*. It was Cowley who, in 1932, managed an invitation to the Gregorys for a three-month stay at Yaddo, the artists' colony in Saratoga Springs, New York. By then their second child, Patrick, had been born. The children were cared for by day in a lodging house in Saratoga, and Zaturenska had a productive period. Over the years, she was to write several poems about Yaddo itself, most notably "House of Chimeras."

It was during her first stay at Yaddo that Zaturenska made what she felt was her creative breakthrough. Despite the fact that her earliest poems had been readily accepted by good magazines, and that she had won a prize, her critical instinct had prevented her from rushing into print with a book. Gregory by now had published two volumes, a new English version of Catullus's poems and his own first collection, *Chelsea Rooming House*. It was another Wisconsin professor, Moses Slaughter, who had encouraged Gregory's translating Horace and Catullus. His early poems set the tone for much of his subsequent poetry, a series of dramatic monologues composed in free verse that were remarkably modern for their time. *The Dictionary of Literary Biography* called *Chelsea Rooming House* "one of the most impressive first books by any modern American poet."

In September of that year, 1932, Zaturenska recorded in her diary, "I want to write. I feel as if slowly, painfully, quietly, I'm finding my medium. And for the first time in years I do not feel hopeless and ashamed of my own poetry; a slow feeling of creation and achievement is coming into my blood, and I feel as if I'm discovering a pure articulate line that will be good if I can only keep on developing and writing" (entry for Sept. 29, 1932).

Harriet Monroe for some time had been encouraging Zaturenska to put together a book, as had Mark Van Doren. But she had resisted, citing unreadiness, the smallness of her children, her distressing circumstances during the Depression, the lack of time. But the gift of three months at Yaddo enabled her to assemble her first book, *Threshold and Hearth*. Monroe and Van Doren were editors at Macmillan, the publishers of Hardy and Yeats, as well as Edwin Arlington Robinson, John Masefield, Ruth Pitter, and Marianne Moore. Macmillan accepted her book, and it was published in 1934. Poems like "The Narrow Hemisphere" revealed Zaturenska's genius; it is simple in form, but rich in music and meaning. That same year, she and Gregory made the first of three trips to England and Ireland (returning again in 1939 and 1951). A meeting was arranged with Yeats in Dublin on the first of these. At the last minute, Zaturenska showed her characteristic modesty, and took their daughter, Joanna, to the movies instead, leaving her husband alone with Yeats at the Kildare Street Club (H. Gregory 1971, 252–53). No matter; she would soon receive the Shelley Award for Poetry in 1935 and the Guarantor's Prize in 1936.

After such a critical reception, Macmillan naturally was interested in her second volume, *Cold Morning Sky.* It was published in 1937—the same year as publication of new collections by Ezra Pound, Wallace Stevens, Edna St. Vincent Millay, Robinson Jeffers, e. e. cummings, Allen Tate, Sara Teasdale, and Louise Bogan. Zaturenska received the Pulitzer Prize. When she answered the telephone call from a Columbia University official, she thought it was her prankster friend, the novelist James T. Farrell, playing another joke, and she refused to believe the news. Her diary entry for May 5, 1938, captures the moment: "Wild excitement—telephones—telegrams—champagne and roses . . . Joanna acting as secretary . . . Pat firing off his toy pistols without knowing what it was all about."

What it was all about was the high point of her writing career. She was just thirty-six. Of the Pulitzer winners for 1938, she was the youngest. But it was her husband whose career proved to be the more honored. Eventually, he was elected to the American Institute of Arts and Letters; she was not. He received the Bollingen Prize for Poetry, perhaps our highest poetry award; she did not. One reason was that his verse was more "modern"—unrhymed free verse using contemporary images and terminology.

In September 1935, the Gregorys moved to Bronxville, New York, to be closer to Sarah Lawrence College, where Gregory had been given a teaching position on the basis of his books. He conducted a poetry hour once a week and in alternate years lectured on classical literature in translation and seventeenth-century literature. In addition, his early college schedule included a writing course titled "Observation and Writing."

In Bronxville, they had a seven-room house. Its open spaces made Zaturenska happy and productive. They left Bronxville in 1938 and lived in New York City on Riverside Drive until 1942, when they moved again, this time to Palisades, New York, a village on the Hudson. Here they lived in a charming pre-Revolutionary War house, white with turquoise shutters, surrounded by a picket fence. Day lilies and roses proliferated in the garden.

One reason for leaving the city probably was to provide a better setting and better schools for the two children. But Patrick Gregory, in his introduction to his mother's published diaries, speaks of her psychological health. At this period in her life, she suffered phobias, among them a fear of crossing streets and a reluctance to venture away from home without company. The small park across from their New York apartment, instead of being a haven, had "become a prison" according to her diary (Zaturenska 2000, entry for 1942). A poem such as her "Afternoon of a Doll," for all its portraiture of childhood innocence, is counterpointed by "shrieking auto horns," "traffic lights / Red, green, green, red," and "harsh voices rising from the city." The move to Palisades gave her more open spaces, no urban traffic, and a change of scene. After reading her diaries in 1998 and 1999, Patrick Gregory concluded, "She was clearly close to a breakdown when she moved to Palisades—and the move did prove beneficial" (Gregory 199d).

Once Joanna was married and Patrick away in boarding school, the Gregorys returned to New York, renting first in Greenwich Village and later returning to Riverside Drive. They had felt the need to get back to the city—for professional reasons and because the commute from Palisades to Sarah Lawrence was becoming a terrible physical strain. They retained the cottage and returned to it in the mid-1950s. Original paintings by their friend e. e. cummings adorned the walls. Shelves were filled with books from their lifetimes of collecting and reviewing. Books lined the stairway and even the attic. Many were inscribed by friends—Samuel Beckett, Dame Edith Sitwell, Robert Lowell, Robinson Jeffers, William Carlos Williams, and H. D., among others.

After *Cold Morning Sky,* there would be six more collections of her poems published in this country, including a *Selected Poems* and a *Collected Poems,* as well as a seventh volume issued by Botteghe Oscure in Italy. Her *Selected Poems* was a finalist for the 1955 National Book Award. (The judges gave it to Wallace Stevens for his *Collected Poems,* and issued a special citation to e. e. cummings for his *Poems, 1923–1954.* Zaturenska was pleased to see cummings honored.) She won the Jacob Gladstein Award from *Poetry* magazine for a group of poems published in 1973, including the memorable "Bird and the Muse." This was fifty-three years after her first appearance in the magazine.

In 1977, both she and her husband were given honorary doctorate degrees from the University of Wisconsin. Now confined to a wheelchair, Gregory could not make the trip because of ill health, but Zaturenska attended, marching in her cap and gown. ("There aren't honors enough in this world, and I'm going to get mine!" she told me.) She received a standing ovation, and afterward dined with the governor. Her citation read in part, "For her creative and distinctive contributions to American poetry which have won national acclaim, for her significant and influential works in the fields of biography, literary criticism, and history."

In 1979, both she and Gregory received Ingram Merrill Awards of six thousand dollars. This award was not something for which one could apply. Throughout their careers, the Gregorys made a point not to apply for grants, although Horace did apply for a Guggenheim in 1934 (M. Z. diary entry for Feb. 19, 1931).

Once Zaturenska found her characteristic voice and mode in the late 1930s, she never abandoned them, a practice for which she received both praise and abuse over the decades. On the positive side, in reviewing her *Collected Poems* in 1969, poet-critic Kenneth Fields wrote in the *Southern Review,* "The difficulty is that she is a literary poet, and the conventions she invokes have for some time been out of favor, and the poets themselves no longer read. . . . The difficulty with Miss Zaturenska's work is that although her antecedents are chiefly second-rate, she is a writer of great talent. Except for a few poems by Christina Rossetti, Miss Zaturenska is considerably better than her elders" (1969, 577). Zaturenska's diaries make it clear that the poets she most respected were Dante, Rilke, Vaughan, Herbert, Hardy, Landor, Leopardi, Rossetti, and Pope—hardly "second-raters." Perhaps Fields means that Zaturenska was not much influenced by the critically fashionable poetry of her own time, which is true. How she must have relished the invocation of Christina Rossetti, who was one of the poets she most admired. The other was Emily Dickinson. "Both of these women kept an inner purity and intensity and a disregard for everything but the final truth that they found in a rich inner life," she told one interviewer (Phillips 1978, 42).

In a favorable review in *Poetry* of her last volume, *The Hidden Waterfall* (1974), Robert B. Shaw spoke of her lack of venturousness throughout her career. "Such consistency may be a virtue, but it is not a trait which characterizes the lifework of our greatest poets who master one technique only to advance to another more demanding" (1975, 100). To which I can imagine Zaturenska quoting Oscar Wilde in reply, "Only mediocrities develop!"

Many of our best critics supported Zaturenska's aesthetic. In an important essay in the *Saturday Review of Literature,* Louis Untermeyer wrote, "Her poetry is like no other writing on either side of the Atlantic. Without limiting herself to a program, the poetry is distinctly of these times and yet occupied with a sense of timelessness. . . . In spirit as well as substance this half-musing, half-singing verse has a form of its own, a pure shape rare at any time, rarer than ever today" (1941). Barbara Guest, reviewing Zaturenska's career in 1965 in the *New York Times Book Review,* said she "upholds the acclaim that has been given her, and even surpasses it. . . . It must be said that rarely has this prize [the Pulitzer] recognized poetry of such delicacy and grace" (62). One thinks of Zaturenska's image, "Love, like an avalanche, destroying me," from the early "For the Seasons."

Harold Witt, writing in Karl Shapiro's *Prairie Schooner,* said of *Terraces of Light:* "Opening the book to any page is to be in the presence of one whose technique is flawless. She never falters or hesitates, and each poem has a music that seems to be entangled in the subject or mood itself. The voice is a distinct one, her own, and always exquisitely lyrical" (1960).

In the late 1970s, the Gregorys decided to move to Shelburne Falls, Massachusetts, to be near their son. Horace Gregory needed assistance to and from a wheelchair, and Zaturenska was finding that she no longer could manage him and the house. It was in Shelburne Falls that they died within months of one another, she first on January 19, 1982, he on March 9. Both deaths were reported in the *New York Times,* Zaturenska's obituary appearing with a photograph.

No discussion of Zaturenska's career is complete without mentioning her prose works, those written alone and those written in collaboration with her husband. Her premier prose work is *Christina Rossetti: A Portrait with Background* (1949). It is a vivid portrayal of the poet's life and mind and her peculiar withdrawal from the Pre-Raphaelite poets and artists of whom her brother, Dante Gabriel Rossetti, was leader, as well as a full discussion of the strengths of her work. The opening paragraph is typical of Zaturenska's prose, which supports her claim that the book not only is criticism, but also provides a "background":

> In 1832 a milkman paid his morning call on a small shabby house in London. The address was 38 Charlotte Street, near Portland Place. It had once been a rather fashionable neighborhood; Samuel Rogers, the banker poet, had lived there and the houses when new had worn an air of fresh, bright Regency elegance. But the neighborhood had sunk, the atmosphere was now one of genteel poverty, of poverty that had long given up any pretensions to being anything else but poverty. The milkman had noticed Number 38: foreigners

lived there—Italians—and the atmosphere was respectable and yet very odd. Even the children seemed "different," and today they were more peculiar than ever. There, in the long dark corridor, a hazel-eyed boy of about four was sitting before a hobby horse and carefully sketching it. (Zaturenska 1949, 1)

While Zaturenska disclaimed being a scholar, her bibliography of background reading, her use of unpublished letters to and from Dante Gabriel, Christina, and William Rossetti, and her study of Pre-Raphaelite pictures and manuscripts reveal her to have been a very responsible scholar, as well as a balanced one.

She later employed her knowledge of the period to edit *Selected Poems of Christina Rossetti* (1970), a garland that showed all phases of the poet's genius—love poems, devotional poems, nature poems, and children's verses. Zaturenska also edited *Collected Poems of Sara Teasdale* (1966). In her introduction, combining her customary interests in biography, background, and criticism, Zaturenska argues persuasively for the resemblance of Teasdale's verse to that of Christina Rossetti and compares Teasdale favorably with another modern American lyric poet, Elinor Wylie. A third book she edited was A. C. Swinburne's one completed novel, *Love's CrossCurrents* (1964). At one time Swinburne was a passion of hers, and one can see why—his rhythmical subtlety and variations, coupled with vast emotional energy, are not unlike some of Zaturenska's own poems. Unlike Zaturenska's, Swinburne's lyrics such as *Dolores* went out of control and displayed sexual immaturity. At one point, Zaturenska had half-completed a book-length study of Swinburne, but she ceased work on it, saying, "I'm not wild about Swinburne anymore. Aside from his poetry, he had no life." Then she added, "And yet, on second thought, no life is without meaning. Swinburne did have a crazy romantic splendor" (Phillips 1978, 46).

Her interest in poets' lives as well as their work manifested itself in the volume she coauthored with Horace Gregory. *A History of American Poetry, 1900–1940* was originally published in 1946 and reprinted with a new foreword in 1969. At the time it originally appeared, historical criticism was out of fashion. The Gregorys began anew, looking at forgotten poets, including William Vaughan Moody, Joaquin Miller, George Santayana, and Adelaide Crapsey, among many others. The decades following publication confirmed the Gregorys' taste. Among those they had cited who increased in influence and favor were Hart Crane, W. H. Auden, Wallace Stevens, Robinson Jeffers, e. e. cummings, and Weldon Kees. It was a true history, useful even today because it provides a background for the present poetry scene.

The Gregorys were naïve, however. They did not foresee the rancor they would create by eliminating living poets or speaking of them unfavorably. They dethroned Mark Van Doren and damned Conrad Aiken, and they called Laura Riding "an industrious, earnest, and ungifted amateur" (Gregory and Zaturenska 1946, 381). And so on. The reaction was deafening. Delmore Schwartz's review, titled "An Intolerable Confusion," took up three pages of the *Nation* and began, "It is difficult to say how much is wrong with this book because there is so much that is wrong and the wrongness is of so many different kinds" (Schwartz 1946, 660). Of Schwartz they had written that his "promise was more in evidence than [his] achievement," and that he carried with him some few of the flaws and merits of the generation that preceded him. They concluded that in his criticism and in his poetry, "Schwartz has followed a style that has been acceptable to the editors of the *Southern Review*" (Gregory and Zaturenska 1946, 495). In the end, the Gregorys had the last laugh. Their *History* is still used today.

Zaturenska collaborated with her husband on two other books, both anthologies: *The Crystal Cabinet: An Invitation to Poetry* (1962) and *The Silver Swan: Poems of Romance and Mystery* (1966). They were fresh and wide-ranging selections, reflecting the Gregorys' lifetimes of reading, as well as their tastes and judgment. "Give a young person the right poems to read and he will naturally appreciate whatever is good," Zaturenska once said (Phillips 1978, 39).

That totals seven critical works, editions, and anthologies, not including the appearance of her diaries simultaneously with the present *New Selected Poems.* Two prose works remain to be put into print (excluding the uncompleted Swinburne study). The first is cast as fiction—six chapters on her childhood in Russia. The second is *A Gallery of Poets,* essays on sixteen favorite poets. The writers are Thomas Campion, John Donne, Lord Herbert of Cherbury, Robert Herrick, George Herbert, Richard Lovelace, Henry Vaughan, Alexander Pope, Thomas Moore, Robert Browning, Christina Rossetti, Emily Dickinson, William Morris, Swinburne, Teasdale, and Dame Edith Sitwell. It was announced as forthcoming from her last publisher, Vanguard Press, but ultimately they declined the manuscript, telling the poet they "didn't know how to market such a book." Crushed, Zaturenska gave the

manuscript to friends in New York City and never again attempted to find a
publisher. The manuscript only recently has surfaced.

Notwithstanding all this, Zaturenska should be remembered primarily for
her poetry and translations. She is one of a handful of American modernists
who were true lyric poets. Of the three general categories of poetic litera-
ture—narrative, dramatic, and lyric—none is so difficult to achieve and sustain
for the length of a poem, or a career, than the lyric. This difficulty is due to the
genre's apparent emotional spontaneity and musical qualities. Most successful
lyrical poetry is brief, metrical, subjective, passionate, sensual, and highly
imagistic. All those terms apply to the best of Zaturenska's work. Her poems
seem more substantial than Sara Teasdale's, less opaque than Léonie Adams's,
and more consistent than Edna St. Vincent Millay's. When Zaturenska assem-
bled her *Collected Poems,* she deleted her few war poems, saying they were not
good enough, and she hated politics—having run away with her parents from
the Russian Revolution and having lived through the Depression (Phillips
1978, 45). She never collected her group of poems on John Reed, whose
short life as a revolutionary writer and activist made him the hero of a genera-
tion of radical intellectuals—despite the fact that these poems were awarded
the John Reed Memorial Prize from *Poetry* in 1924. Her best war poem, "The
Unsepulchred," however, is included in this volume, as is "Lullaby," from the
late 1930s, with its forebodings of dark changes in the world.

Like Zaturenska, Millay was a prodigy. Her famous "Renascence" was
published when she was scarcely nineteen. Many of her sonnets are first rate.
But she went on to write an entire book of antiwar poems of a journalistic fa-
cility *(Make Bright the Arrows,* 1940), and a second collection on Czechoslo-
vakian terrorism *(The Murder of Lidice,* 1942). Other lyric poets have sullied
their reputations as lyric poets by succumbing to the political soap box, more
recently Muriel Rukeyser and Denise Levertov. Zaturenska was wise to weed
the political from her garden.

I have mentioned only women lyric poets. The American lyric poet in the
first half of this century who must not be denied is Robert Frost, yet he is not
always labeled a lyric poet, perhaps because he also wrote narrative poems and
verse plays.

The poet with whom Zaturenska might best be compared is Louise
Bogan. Like Zaturenska's lyrics, Bogan's reveal a keen intellect and a
metaphorical bent. Both wrote lyrics that are compact and infused with a per-
sonal vision. Although far less consistent, Zaturenska was more spontaneous

and positive than Bogan. Of the two, it is Bogan who has been taken up by re-
cent critics. In their efforts to redress the absence of American woman poets in
the canon, contemporary critics have tended to focus on Bogan and Elizabeth
Bishop. Bishop is not primarily a lyric poet, although she has written a fine vil-
lanelle ("One Art") and a sonnet that is not formally a sonnet. Technically and
vocally, Bishop's work is closest to that of her mentor, Marianne Moore, who
wrote in syllabics, not meter and rhyme. While Zaturenska did not always
rhyme, she felt poetry without music was like painting without color. And
how she used color! The poem "Places" is full of red, blue, and gold.

    I would suggest that the canon is not yet closed, and that students and crit-
ics might be rewarded by taking a close look at Zaturenska. Beneath the con-
ventional surface of her work, there are emotional depths to be plumbed. Part
of the fascination lies at the source of many of her poems, strange and secret
sources coming from dreams, the subconscious, or supernatural inspiration,
the "underseas of floating memory," as she said in "The Island." She once
spoke of having strong psychic experiences, especially after moving to her his-
torical house in Rockland County (Phillips 1978, 39). Poems like "The White
Dress," "The Séance," "Four Ghosts," "The Uninvited Guest," "House of
Chimeras," and "The Haunted House" all have a supernatural strain. Her best
work seems a combination of acute observation and shadowy allegory, music
and parable. When she read her poems in public, it was as if she went into a
trance. The only contemporary reader who is comparable is Louise Glück.

    Other themes are poverty, spirituality, history, love, friendship, and child-
hood. Three of her finest poems, "Night Music," "Another Snowfall," and
"The Castaways," champion the underdog or the insecure. ("The Castaways"
was greatly admired by W. H. Auden, and at his going-away party at the Cof-
fee House Club in Manhattan in 1972, just before he moved to Christ Church
College in Oxford, Zaturenska was seated at his right-hand side.) Zaturenska
found beauty in modest or diminished things, as in "Song" and one of her
finest poems, "The Daisy." This is in direct opposition to many of the latter-
day poets of High Culture (James Merrill, Anthony Hecht, J. D. McClatchy),
who write of operas and European art and artifacts.

    When asked to name the most beautiful word in the English language,
Henry James responded, "Youth!" Zaturenska may have felt similarly. In her
last book, *The Hidden Waterfall,* published when she was seventy-two, three
poems are titled "A Young Girl's Singing," "The Young Dancers," and "O
Like a Young Tree."

She could be an inspiration to the so-called New Formalists of today. This movement has flourished for two decades, since the early 1980s. Although its practitioners write in traditional forms, their work varies from their formal predecessors in the modernity of their subject matter. One cannot imagine a Zaturenska or a Millay writing a sonnet about abortion or premenstrual syndrome, as the New Formalists do. I could argue that New Formalism is a misnomer, that the old formalism never went away: Richard Wilbur, William Jay Smith, James Merrill, John Hollander, Anthony Hecht, Carolyn Kizer, Isabella Gardner, and legions of others continued to write formal lyrics during and after the Beats, Naked Poetry, Objectivism, Language Poetry, Hip-Hop poetry, what have you. But it is their new subject matter within old forms that makes the New Formalists new. Lyrical poetry no longer has to be written about lyrical moments. I am reminded of Zaturenska's *Modern Poetry Studies* interview. When asked what she thought about what was happening in American poetry, she replied, "I feel like a nun who has walked into a rock-and-roll festival" (Phillips 1978, 43).[1]

New Formalists might well look at Zaturenska's variations with meter and often-subtle sounds. In "Hymn to Artemis, the Destroyer," for instance, she makes splendid use of internal and concealed rhyme. In "Cold Morning Sky" the music is enriched by such slant effects as pairing *breath* with *sheath,* and *done* with *dawn.* In "Image of a Friend" she links *mind* and *wind.* In "The Virgin, the Doe and the Leper," a poem with an *abab* rhyme scheme, she breaks the pattern at the end of the fourth line of the fourth stanza to emphasize the word *bleeds.* While she used forms, Zaturenska was not a slave to them, which is why her work is musical but does not jangle. There is considerable influence of fine music on her poetry—not only meter, but various musical forms. Many of her poems' titles contain the word *song, chorale, variations,* and *hymn.* On the other hand, she was almost equally fascinated with the phenomenon of silence, hence "Quiet Countries," "The Interpreter of Silence," and "Silence and the Wayfarer."

For the most part, her imagery could be described as lovely, though one

---

1. Because the New Formalists embrace narrative storytelling as well as traditional forms, the movement also is known as Expansive Poetry. Its practitioners include Dana Gioia, Molly Peacock, R. S. Gwynn, and Mary Jo Salter. (Those interested in this development in post-World War II American poetry are directed to Kevin Walzer's *Ghost of Tradition: Expansive Poetry and Postmodernism,* 1998.)

finds lepers, vultures, wrestlers, arrows, javelins, swords, and other unlovely things in her poems. In her introduction to a book devoted to the sculpture of Doris Caesar, Zaturenska addressed what she called the "problem" of the limited achievement of women in the arts (Zaturenska 1970a, 21). She lamented that there were so few women in musical composition or even painting. (In the former category, she might have mentioned Mrs. Amy Beach, Dame Ethel Smyth, and Clara Schuman; in the latter, Mary Cassatt, Georgia O'Keefe, Louise Nevelson, Louise Bourgoise, and Frida Kahlo might be evoked.) She did cite, in literature, Jane Austen, Emily Bronté, Colette, and Anna Akhmatova—all solid choices. She made clear the characteristics she admired most in a woman's art: "An unmistakable feminine sensibility and strength, a touch of pathos, an inner intensity" (21–22). Surely, these are characteristics of her own poetry. No one would ever think them written by a man, although today the statement sounds sexist.

All her poems are relatively brief, as true lyrics are. In her *Modern Poetry Studies* interview, she said, "It requires great art to do the marvelous short poem. As someone else has said, 'People write long poems, lacking the skill to write short ones.' " She reminded us that Ezra Pound wrote, "Poetry begins to atrophy when it gets too far from the Muse" (Phillips 1978, 41). She did on occasion write a longer poetic sequence (as opposed to a sustained long poem). One is "A Shakespearean Cycle." Another is the eight-poem sequence "Leaves from the Book of Dorothy Wordsworth," which for some reason she omitted from her *Collected Poems*. I gladly restore it to print here.

Another aspect of her work worth examining is the immediacy of her first lines. She most often plunges the reader straight into the poem: "Imperceptively the world became haunted by her white dress . . ." "How long she waited for her executioner! . . ." etc.

What follows is a personal selection. Doubtless other readers would produce a very different table of contents. If one compares my selections with those that Zaturenska (and perhaps her husband) made for her *Selected Poems* of 1954 and her *Collected Poems* of 1965, it will be clear that I have not included many of the poems the poet herself preferred, and I have included a number she herself did not select for those volumes. My object has been to display the poet in all her phases. If there were many lyrics on the seasons, for instance, I tried to select the best. I found much more variety than some critics have been willing to concede. I also came to appreciate that her final book,

The Hidden Waterfall, may have been her finest, most controlled single collection, especially in its cycle of Shakespearean lyrics.

The present volume consists of 126 poems and 20 translations, a total of 146 works drawn from eight books—including a handful of early and uncollected poems, to show her development and also her precocity. Of the "juvenilia," one might apply to Zaturenska what T. S. Eliot said of William Blake, only changing the gender: "The early poems show what the poems of a [girl of] genius ought to show, immense power of assimilation" (Eliot 1960, 276). Saturated in both the grim reality of tenement life in New York City and the magical enchantment of her reading, the young Zaturenska yearned for physical and psychological release.

The excellent translations reveal both the breadth of her sympathies and her metrical versatility. As noted, she sometimes wrote without rhyme, but almost never without meter. Music was the key. Her translations have been admired by Ezra Pound and other expert translators including William Jay Smith and Dana Gioia. In her interview, she stated that her interest in translation stemmed from Dante Gabriel Rossetti's translations of the Renaissance Italian poets: "I began to translate when I began to love a certain poem and wished to reproduce it perfectly in English. I believe that a good poem in any language should be as good an English poem as it was in the original language" (Phillips 1978, 45).

The poems published here are those selected by the poet for the eight collections published during her lifetime, with the exception of the few early and uncollected ones. The volumes themselves are represented in chronological order, but I have taken the liberty of changing the arrangement of poems drawn from each. Except for a few, all titles are the poet's own.

I have silently corrected errors of spelling that crept into magazine and book appearances of the poems, and I have standardized spelling in cases where Zaturenska sometimes used the English rather than the American spelling. I have resisted the temptation to add punctuation where I sometimes felt it was necessary, particularly in the early poems, where Zaturenska would sometimes let a line break stand for the period at the end of a sentence. I am mindful of the misrepresentation of Emily Dickinson's work by "editors" who removed her dashes. Zaturenska began to use more conventional punctuation from *The Listening Landscape* (1941) forward.

I have combined Zaturenska's translations and adaptations to form the book's final section, and I have standardized their titles. In addition, I have combined the two fragments from her poem-in-progress, "The Madness of Jean Jacques Rousseau"—published thirty years apart—to make one poem, something she agreed to do upon publication of *The Hidden Waterfall* in 1974 but which somehow did not come to pass. That work is placed with her last poems. A few poems were published in more than one volume. They appear here under the title of the book in which they first appeared.

Zaturenska's admirers may think 139 poems and translations an insufficient representation, but I think she would approve. In her diary entry for July 1, 1935, she wrote, "I must build a monument against time. And all that must be done with no thought, no hope, of fame or publication, but in the hope that something out of it, say 3 poems out of a hundred, will be worth something, will deserve to endure, will prove that my life was not useless." Such were her standards—three poems out of a hundred.

Of Marya Zaturenska one could say what she herself wrote about Sara Teasdale: "Though she is not among the names most mentioned in fashionable reviews, her poems seem secure among the noises of present controversy and changing techniques. One has a feeling that as time passes she will endure in some clear atmosphere of her own, when many better-known names are forgotten or are merely footnotes to literary history" (Zaturenska 1966, xvii). Or, as Kenneth Fields wrote in the *Southern Review,* "As long as it is considered a virtue to write beautiful and intelligent poems, Miss Zaturenska's work should be read" (Fields 1969, 578).

•   •   •

In the preparation of this volume, the editor is grateful to Patrick B. Gregory and Mary Beth Hinton. Melanie Malinowski originally reproduced the text. Gregory Fraser rescued the entire book from succumbing to a computer virus. And for spiritual support, I thank Dr. Eric L. Brown.

Robert Phillips

Works Cited

Contemporary Authors, new rev. ser. 1979. Vol. 22, 519–20. Detroit: Gale Research Inc.
Contemporary Literary Criticism. 1976. Vol. 6, 585–86. Detroit: Gale Research Inc.

Eliot, T. S. 1960. "William Blake." In *Selected Essays,* 275–80. New York: Harcourt, Brace and World.

Fields, Kenneth. 1969. "J. V. Cunningham and Others." Review of *Collected Poems. Southern Review* 5, no. 2: 577–78.

Gregory, Horace. 1956. "Introduction." In *The Poems of Catullus,* translated by Horace Gregory, v-xxiv. New York: Grove Press.

———. 1971. *The House on Jefferson Street: A Cycle of Memories.* New York: Holt, Rinehart and Winston.

———. 1978. "Guest Editor." *Poetry Pilot,* Jan 9.

Gregory, Horace, and Marya Zaturenska. 1946. *A History of American Poetry, 1900–1940.* New York: Harcourt, Brace and World.

Gregory, Patrick. 1999a. Letter to Robert Phillips, Jan. 22.

———. 1999b. Letter to Robert Phillips, Feb. 1.

———. 1999c. Letter to Robert Phillips, Feb. 3.

———. 1999d. Letter to Robert Phillips, May 24.

Guest, Barbara. 1965. "Bright Passions." Review of *Collected Poems. New York Times Book Review,* Nov. 28, 62.

Kunitz, Stanley J., and Vineta Coldy. 1951. *Twentieth Century Authors: A Biographical Dictionary of Modern Literature. First Supplement,* 1570. New York: H. W. Wilson.

Phillips, Robert. 1975. "A True Lyric Poet." Review of *The Hidden Waterfall. Ontario Review,* no. 1: 98–100.

———. 1978. "The Real Thing: An Interview with Marya Zaturenska." *Modern Poetry Studies* 9, no. 1: 33–46.

———. 1990. "Visiting the Gregorys." *The New Criterion* 20, no. 1: 24–34.

———. 1991. "Featured Poet." *Poetry Pilot,* Apr. 5, 71.

———. Forthcoming. *The Madness of Art: Interviews with Poets & Writers.* Syracuse: Syracuse Univ. Press.

Schwartz, Delmore. 1946. "An Intolerable Confusion." *The Nation,* Dec. 7, 660, 662, 664.

Shaw, Robert B. 1975. "Courtly Music." *Poetry* 126:100–102.

Untermeyer, Louis. 1938. "The Pulitzer Prize Winners." Review of *Cold Morning Sky. Saturday Review of Literature,* May 7, 12.

———. 1941. "Verse of the Times." Review of *The Listening Landscape. Saturday Review of Literature,* April 5, 30–31.

———. 1950. "Marya Zaturenska." *Modern American Poetry,* mid-century ed. Edited by Louis Untermeyer, 599–603. New York: Harcourt, Brace.

Walzer, Kevin. *The Ghost of Tradition: Expansive Poetry and Postmodernism.* Ashland, Oreg.: Story Line Press.

Zaturenska, Marya. 1949. *Christina Rossetti: A Portrait with Background*. New York: Macmillan.

———. 1966. "The Strange Victory of Sara Teasdale." In *Collected Poems of Sara Teasdale*, xvii-xxxii. New York: Collier.

———. 1968–86. Letters to Robert Phillips. The Horace Gregory Collection, Syracuse University Library, Department of Special Collections, Syracuse, N.Y.

———. 1970a. "Introduction." *Doris Caesar*, by Martin H. Bush, 21–22. Syracuse, N.Y. Distributed by Syracuse Univ. Press.

———. 1970b. "The Passionate Austerity of Christina Rossetti." In *Selected Poems of Christina Rossetti*, 3–17. New York: Macmillan.

———. 1996. "Marya Zaturenska's Depression Diary, 1932–33." Introduction by Mary Beth Hinton. *Syracuse University Library Associates Courier* 31: 129–52.

———. 2000. "Marya Zaturenska's Depression Diary, 1933–35." Introduction by Mary Beth Hinton. *Syracuse University Library Associates Courier* 33.

———. 2001. The Diaries of *Marya Zaturenska, 1938–1944*. Edited by Mary Beth Hinton. Syracuse: Syracuse Univ. Press.

• • •

Early and Uncollected Poems

1920–1933

• • •

Spinners

SHE LONGS FOR THE COUNTRY

It is the May-time now,
And in a place I know
Some girl God will allow
To see the cowslips blow;

And the hyacinths, the fern
That grow by the riversides;
Narcissi, white and stern
Like sad unwilling brides.

Some other girl will run
And, dancing through the grass,
Will laugh in the wholesome sun,
And feel the sweet hours pass.

Laugh! Laugh, and play for me!
Go where the sweet flowers grow,
And see what I cannot see!

THE SPINNERS AT WILLOWSLEIGH

The young girl passes by

The old women sit at Willowsleigh. They spin,
And shriek and sing above the humming din.

They are so very old and brown and wise,
One is afraid to look them in the eyes.

Their bony fingers make a chilly sound,
Like dead bones shaking six feet underground!

Their toothless singing mocks—they seem to say:
"What I was yesterday you are today;

Stars kissed my eyes, the sunlight loved my brow.
You'll be tomorrow what I am now."

They dream and talk—they are so old and lean;
And the whole world is young and fresh and green.

Once they were flowers, and flame, and living bread;
Now they are old and strange, and almost dead!

The old women spin at Willowsleigh; they fool
And scold, and sleep. Once they were beautiful.

SONG OF A FACTORY GIRL

It's hard to breathe in a tenement hall
So I ran to the little park,
As a lover runs from a crowded ball
To the moonlit dark.

I drank in clear air as one will
Who is doomed to die,
Wistfully watching from a hill
The unmarred sky.

And the great trees bowed in their gold and red
Till my heart caught flame;
And my soul, that I thought was crushed or dead,
Uttered a name.

I hadn't called the name of God
For a long time;
But it stirred in me as the seed in sod,
Or a broken rhyme.

A SONG FOR VANISHED BEAUTY

The house is desolate and bare—
So long ago young Honora left
Her quiet chair!

Through the rose-bordered gardens, reft
Of all her pretty, tender care—
The silent hall, the lonely stair—

No one can see her anywhere.
Here is her shawl, her fan, her book—
She is not there.

No one remembers her bright hair,
Or how she looked, or when Death came.
Few can recall her name.

Where shall we turn to hope or look
For beauty vanished like an air?—
In what forgotten tomb or nook?

AN OLD TALE

What shall we say of her,
Who went the path we knew of? She is dead—
What shall we say of her?

Men who are very old
Still speak of her. They say
That she was far too beautiful; they say

Her beauty wrought her ruin. But they
Are very old.

The old wives break their threads, they shake their heads.
They shake their heads when men will speak of her;
They say she was too beautiful.

I must not think of her, I must
Not speak of her! My mother says
One should not think of her.

She went the path we knew of; she is dead.
They say few knew her truly while she lived,
Though men will speak of her.

It really does not matter she is dead.
One need not think of her, although one night
Folks heard her weeping yet beside a pool.
One moonlit springtime I could swear she sang.
But she is dead—one must not think of her.

MEMORIES

Lower New York City at noon hour

There is a noise, and then the crowded herd
Of noon-time workers flows into the street.
My soul, bewildered and without retreat,
Closes its wings and shrinks, a frightened bird.

Oh, I have known a peace, once I have known
The joy that could have touched a heart of stone—
The heart of holy Russia beating still,
Over a snow-cold steppe and on a hill:
One day in Kiev I heard a great church-bell
Crying a strange farewell.

And once in a great field, the reapers sowing
Barley and wheat, I saw a great light growing
Over the weary bowed heads of the reapers;
As growing sweeter, stranger, ever deeper,
From the long waters sorrowfully strong,
Came the last echoes of the River Song.
Here in this alien crowd I walk apart,
Clasping remembered beauty to my heart!

Fulfillment

I have reached Willowsleigh through what strange passes,
Through endless desolations I remembered,
Your sky-swept walks, your bright unearthly flowers.
The City of God, the village known in dreams,
Is mine; I walk the unforgotten grasses.

The seasons pass, the sun stands high and still
as through a crystal my tall neighbors go
Walled in by desolate quiet, bound yet free.
The grass is up, then gone, and spring comes and December;
The heat, the frost, the fragrance, the rain and the snow!

The Girl Takes Her Place Among the Mothers

To link the generations each to each.
—Tennyson

I wake in the night with such uncertain gladness,
Fearing the little pain beneath my heart,
The little pains that cease again and start,
Delicious fear that aches with a strange madness.

"And is this I?" I say, seeing my shadowed face
In the old mirror where I laughing saw

So long ago, beautiful without flaw,
Its delicate young lines, and careless grace.

This pain, these happy pains that seem to blend
In my young blood with old forgotten mothers,
Daughters of my race and unremembered others,
The pain that foretells life's beginning and end,

"And is this I," I say, beholding my body's line,
Fragile and young and sweet but not the body I knew,
Now I am drunken with the ancient wine—
"Child, as it was with others, so with you."

They Pass

CLOCK-BEAT, HEART-BEAT

To hear the clock strike, and strike away, in a still room,
Is to know Time alive. The house grows veins, knows blood;
Its windows change to eyes; the doors learn breath.
Outside the trains roar on from far away.

In a quiet house the footsteps ring like silver;
In tune with the clock-beat, the feet return—
The young, the delicate, the small, the gay,
The feet dragged home in pain.

So from speed to silence we are united by the clock's beat—
Time winds its little pulse and purrs away.
Heart-beat, clock-beat, we cease to measure them—
I turn with patience the worn leaves of the day.

SYMBOLS

Only by these old symbols do I move,
And by these ancient symbols do I die:

The spreading tree, the rock on the worn hill,
The moonbeam spent by love,
The roots in the poor soil, the heart
In the sick flesh, the bone
In the lost skeleton.
Oh, why so still, my song?
Leave the eternal pastoral and fly
To where the city's vast metallic eye
Opens on visions carved of iron and steel,
Machinery too immaculate to feel
The silent drop of blood beneath the stone.

OATH ON AN ALTAR

By those unfeeling eyes,
Emasculated, luminous, precise,
I swear to steep my soul in brightest ice,
And walk through oceans, valleys, altitudes,
That rise and sink and change and die forever.

By those forgotten hands,
I make my vow, old love, deep buried now
By what forsaken altar, and what shrine
Made sacred by the goat-feet of a god.
I loosen veils of darkness, I shall bathe
In sunlight of your memory, that fades
And leaves a shadow brighter than the sun.

Oh, be obscured,
My passionate one, be buried and lie hidden—
My love feeds on the hidden roots of time.
Let rumor hide your eyes, pity your hands,
And terror shield you with her coverlet,
While your bright sword is sleeping with the worm.

The Empress Marie Louise

She had slept with greatness, and its shadows troubled
That light and facile head, so soft and pretty.
"I am tired," she said, "of empires and of battles,
I am tired of the great bed with its golden eagles,
Tired of the god who became man to me,
Who from my mystical blood would be creating
Eagles and heroes for eternity.

"The drums beat in my boudoir—oh, in light gardens,
In little alcoves let me ease my breast!
Let the great world be whispered like a dream,
Let me wear pink gowns and little muslin sashes
For the limp eyes of fools, and let me lie
In some knave's arms, with words of soft surrender,
Far from the great king whose prize I was.
I was his prize; when his great throne shall fall,
I shall dissolve, I shall be the mist and the air,
And be inviolable beyond his call.

"I brought corruptions in my pleasant breasts,
Though they were pregnant with the breath of life.
Now he has taken Death to be his wife—
I see his silver laurels sink in foam,
His empire lie like thunder undersea.

"I can return to my ancestral home!"

Places

How red the roses were
In that narrow lane
Where we used to meet,
Met and met again.

I see you sitting there
On a stone stair.
On your golden hair
Fell the enamoured air.

The roses were too red
At our cottage door;
Warm light covered the floor,
Flowed and spread.

The ivy was too black,
The roses were too red.
They withered on the stem—
How I remember them.

Do you remember too?
The sky was far too blue.
Your eyes were far bluer.
(They alone were true.)

We wandered by the sea
Led by a lucky star
Known to antiquity.
How good to breathe the air.

I tired of the cottage wall,
The oak tree, and the yew,
Tired of the falling snow,
There was no place to go.

Tired of the blue and green,
The cold rain and the dew,
The winding, vanishing scene—
Tired of all things but you.

·   ·   ·

From "Threshold and Hearth"

1934

•   •   •

Pilgrimage

The wind came up from the black streets my childhood knew
And talked to me although I closed my ears,
Although I wept and turned away my head,
The terrible streets spoke to me of the dead.

They come with the roar of the winds, they are not dead
They bring the lost child back, they torture her,
Their hands are red with her sharp blood, their feet
Thunder in dread irrevocable beat.

What do you wish to say to me O Lost?
(And the trees darken and the houses dwindle)
Stagnation entered my brain and the leaves are twisted with death
I have been blighted by an early frost.

This pilgrimage wise God you marked for me
My life is your cruel map, my goal you traced
In what dim beat of my blood, and in what ring
Of some forgotten, unforgetting thing?

[for Lewis Mumford]

Strange Captivity

Never will you depart
Though often cast away,
Unburied in my heart
Wraithlike you stray.

First, tenuous and thin,
Then warmer, closer, deep,
You pierce without, within,
You enter in my sleep.

And higher, higher, till
My blood calms all my breath,
Your resolute, strong will
Leaps through the walls of death.

Spectre, whose radiant eyes
Destroy all life in me,
Let me immortalize
My strange captivity

In thoughts that none will read,
In blood that leaves no stain,
Words spoken to the rain,
Devotion none will heed.

Reflections on a Centaur

The years grow small and gray
Above the immobile hills,
I see them float away—

Neither have I grown rich,
Or deeper, more serene:
I am what I have been.

Drink, then, with vivid eyes
This brief and changing world
Of morning light and skies;

Observe this marble faun
Whose cool archaic head
Shines out across the lawn—

Mosaic of my blood,
Of each experience,
Carve something large and good.

So will the lost years fly
Nor will I turn, nor heed
Time's centaur, or his speed.
                    [for Horace Gregory]

For the Seasons

Burning with heat and cold
In April's tender weather
I let my tense hands hold
All they could gather of love.

Desire shaking the branch
Of every quivering tree,
Love, like an avalanche,
Destroying me.

Now brightly in the air,
Love's vivid signature
Is more than I can bear,
I bind my flowing hair.

Let other lovers lie
Under that great tree
Of rich incredible fruit
And make their suit:

O turn their burning look
Upon that vast and deep
Starry-lettered book
Whose lovely meanings leap
In generative lore
A moment and no more.

O Lyric March

The cold and violent wind of March
Cuts sharply through this little world
Obscured by the long snow, and a small room
Where quiet melted into gloom.

And then you came yourself, tall lady,
Your hands with fresh flowers, your eyes like birds,
Bright forerunner of song, dispeller of cloud,
Delicate and proud.

Joy for the white arbutus trembling through
The melting, quivering earth and shyly stirring
The shivering tendrils of the grass
To deeper happiness.

Faint mellow sun, O sky too wistful; now
Freshen this little room, this little house
Where iron winter kept too close a guard
In her severest mood,
A marble solitude.

Chorale for Autumn

The leaves of autumn burning through the gray—
Are you dark head, stilled blood and perilous tongue?

Burn O thin trees and in small gardens scatter
Your leaves that on reluctant branches stray.

How many seasons has this tamed heart known
Lashing the hounds of fall to the bare hills
Hallooing among the shadows of a dream
The bright leaves lying where the flowers have been!

Gather the chilled days in, let the calm house
Of peace, entreat, enclose, and comfort them
The days burn cold and high, the sheaves are in
Prepare O Death to hold your last carouse.

The world grows cool as amber and as clear
That which is dark grows light; the sunlight stands
Obscure as anguish worn out by sharp time
As a leaf in its season falls the year.

The Quiet House

Within my house the gray ghost Peace has lain
On a white bed; and strewn about him lay
The agonies I lavendered away
There was a storm once and the rain beat hard,
Besieged by passions I would now discard
I turned to you O house and waited for the world to wane.

Without, within, the pallid walls now wait:
The threshold and the hearth know one command
The windows breathe their life upon my hand,
The gardens hide their knowledge of my fate
No longer lives the urge to run to strive
And I have but to hear and understand
The word that was my spirit's strange unmaking
(I am alive and yet am not alive)
The word that shall loosen the storm and set the still house quaking.

The Narrow Hemisphere

Shall I say the world has narrowed since my youth?
I have seen wide rivers shrink and dry entirely,
I have seen whole gardens lose their fragrant lustre,
I have seen the wild grape falling from its cluster,
While men have talked to me of love and truth.

And poetry withers like a golden fig . . .
Romance has drained my breast like a strong child:
I have known dances, I have known laughter and lover,
I have slept with wisdom under a dark cover,
I have seen the sexton open my grave and dig.

And I have seen old women bowed with living
Trouble the intolerant air with pleas for breath . . .
And I have heard strong, lovely children crying
Their whimsical laughter (while the sick lay dying)
To the old sky their heavenly freshness giving.

Soul's Haven

Because the sterile arms no longer beat
Across the predatory air
But form a cross of grandeur and despair
Because that glorious hair
That grew and flowed like laurel round your head
Lies shorn beneath your feet
Yet I rejoice in my despair, and know
Your agelong summer burning through the snow.

Because your throat no longer holds the word
That shaped the world
Nor your adorable hands the apple of all grace
Yet in all kindness I behold your face
And bless that face and know it mine forever

Safe in your arms across the world's last brink
I stand and hear the coming of the gloom
I learn the slow approach of time and doom.

[for Y. L. Z.]

Daphne

Roots grow from my feet, Apollo, like a tree
The silver laurels grow deep into me
Undone, undone, these thoughts of mine that beat
With a great vigor in the drought and heat
So my blood answers, so with sap my veins,
So as leaves in whom no wind complains
This is the metamorphosis, this the change
Through which my days now range:
That which was I, am now no longer I,
Among my branches let the wild birds cry,
Around me let the alien rivers flow
Beneath my shade let other maidens go.

The Dark Year

The year has become heavy, will you dare
To cast the angelic burden down, forswear
The golden crown whose glory lures you yet
Beyond this world of terror and regret?
Now that the flesh casts silver garments down,
Lays down its wings and feels with darker sight
The grass grows brown at the tips, and it seems night,
Forsake the lovely country for the town.

This is the moment, this is the time to know
When the last roses of your life shall blow
On what strange breast shall be familiar
The coming autumns and the future snow

Retreat into the quiet none shall know
That in my heart I feel the lilies stir.

Image of a Friend

Farewell, clear and profound,
Farewells DeQuincey heard
When mad with drugs and grief,
The quivering of a leaf
Made an iron sound.

O then I knew the flight
Of friendship spun as fine
As light—and rich as wine!
O friend, once mine,
Estranged and grown
Familiarly unknown.

Yet, if in a great book
I wrote her image fair
Or carved it out of air,
She would not look
Who burns with life denied
In her youth's pride
So that her blood is true,
False, cruel, and kind
To one thing in her mind,
The lost April's clue
She follows on the wind.

Her summer dry, and blind,
And winter, winter near,
And death, like a small boy's
Sharp, teasing noise.

The Uninvited Guest

Through what doors will you enter, through what walls
Will your white soul resume its solitudes?
I count the clockbeats in my mind, the warning trumpet
Reechoing in my heart and hear no answer,
No answer and no cry
And no reply.

On a known hour at an appointed rendezvous
(So destiny has spoken)
Your eloquent feet will sing in the dry grass;
I know their rhythm cruel and sweet
And their presaging beat
On that unknown street.

Surprise will come like a stern robber,
Fear like a jealous pain, and a joy
Come carrying gifts disastrous and rich
Yet I shall miss
That steep abyss.

Where shall I wait, where shall impatience lie,
On what low bed of thorns shall my head rest
Until I meet the uninvited guest,
Will the door open at a secret word
Unknown, unheard?

Shall I run down the world whose strict restraint
Held me too long, whose iron hand has left
Its sharp stigmata on my brows and heart
See I have waited long, the golden lamp I light
Through the expectant night.

．　　．　　．

From "Cold Morning Sky"

1938

•   •   •

The Virgin, the Doe and the Leper

They are always there
The frightened virgin at the burning fountain
The leper left upon the fatal stair
The milk-white doe lost on the savage mountain.

Do you not hear them cry?
Despair and shame that final sense
Of doom descending upon innocence
Outcasts from pity's gentle eye?

I fly their shadowy pain
I invoke the guardians of their destiny
Angels of thunder and rain
To keep sick pity from corrupting me.

Earth would deny them
As I deny and plead, earth pleads, denies
"O pitiful, stain not my garment's hem
And hide from me the silent wound that bleeds."

For are we not lost too?
Are we not outcasts from time's living flood?
And often from the sky's deceptive blue
Rains down a shower of blood.

When shelter seemed most near, and love most close
When summer's golden eyelids opened wide

Have we not seen the worm crawl from the rose
Have we not seen the shadowy sisters glide?

Fatal and wan on cherished garden walks
Whose was that sudden cry? that burning chill?
What halts our footsteps? and what stilled our talks?
What shadow stalks us, run wherever we will?

Lullaby

Ruin falls on blackening skies
And disaster lies in wait
For the heart and for the state,
Loud the voices in the street
Shout unhealing remedies.

Sleep, beloved, while you may:
Heralds of the Augustan day
That arise as you awake
Can consume but never slake
The strong thirst, intense and deep,
For the peace that need not sleep.

Let the lion have his hour,
Let the evil beasts devour
Leaf and vine and fruit and flower,
Theirs the night but yours the time
Known to the Vergilian rhyme
When the ancient world, distressed,
Found peace in an infant's breast.

Still remote and gay and young
Sing the stars in ancient peace,
Heralding the great release
In their wordless tongue.
Close your eyes and let them sing

In the morning that will bring
What strange beasts to haunt the spheres?
Revelations? New-found fears?

Let the old world fall away
As the great beasts leave their prey;
Let the dogs and cats destroy
That which they cannot enjoy.
New as life and death and sleep
Shall the cyclic rivers creep,
Bringing learning, art and thought
New again to be renewed,
Revived, restored, and still uncaught,
The intangible pursued.

Sleep, beloved, in the changes
Light from bright to darkness ranges:
Venus, ocean-young, arises,
Love again the earth surprises
Naked, dreaming, peaceful, free,
Springing from the bitter sea
Of unending destiny.

Spring Morning

The arrowy gold whose winter span
Of life was lost in wind and water
Shed from the sky to waters run
Casting new life upon the water.

From water Love herself arose,
Limbs laved in seawater and sun,
Again her smile dissolves the snow
Hearts bared to flowering of the sun.

O brief and glittering time of Joy
When the long thoughts of youth run free
And garlanded the girl and boy
With the young flowers as bright and free.

The dark head and the golden one
Glad in the sun, rose-garlanded
Dream of adventures in the sun
High actions, proud, rose-garlanded.

And from their dreams the laurel grows
While artlessly the tide of love
Circles, expands, contracts, and grows
Through sunlit avenues of love.

The Greek, the natural feet of dawn
Wade in lakewaters, calm the sea
Her footsteps light on the green lawn
Sound like faint signals from the sea.

Gold-streaked the air in luminous flashes
Shadows of trees in water flowing
Nostalgic tears on awakened lashes
Remember joy, its ebbing, flowing.

The Lunar Tides

Danger stalks on such nights, the moon is dangerous:
Why will you walk beneath the compelling lustre
That draws the blood from your unwilling body?
The vampire moon with yellow streams of light
Drains the dim waters, sucks the moist air dry
Casts cloudy spectres on the window pane
The dead arise and walk again.

Oh, Jove how are we drawn
Into this moon, this face as cold
Remorseless as ambition, chilled with fever
Burning with war that on these lunar tides
Draws all life to its danger; beautiful
It mocks the living glory of the sun
Such golden, flowing motion, dipping in perilous play
Forgets the warm assurances of day.

Resistance dies, is plucked so gently from
Our paralyzed wills, we hardly know it gone.
We are surrendered to the moon:
The light compels us, pole-stars to its orbit
We shine in darkness fixed, invisible
Too late for the last withdrawal we are lost
In the intricacies of yellow frost.

Fantasies in the brain, restlessness in the heart
Desire for the unattainable, the pure romantic longing
Ruined towers in the air, a yearning toward the sea
For its deep death, so cool, and languorous
These are the favorite symptoms written down
The pressure of the moon on the rare spirit
The wild attraction, and the deep repulsion
The irresistible compulsion.

Dogs bark invisible terror, the trees loom sharply
These ague glamors shake down mortal ill
The wind beloved by lunatics and lovers
Descends and sways the grass, compels the lost
Dishevelled light as sharp as silver daggers
Such light as never from Olympus poured
But dark Judean light sorrowful pain-extolling
And Christian light, the Gothic thunder rolling.

The Daisy

Having so rich a treasury, so fine a hoard
Of beauty water-bright before my eyes,
I plucked the daisy only, simple and white
In its fringed frock and brooch of innocent gold.

So is all equilibrium restored:
I leave the noontide wealth of richer bloom
To the destroyer, the impatient ravisher,
The intemperate bee, the immoderate bird.

Of all this beauty felt and seen and heard
I can be frugal and devout and plain,
Deprived so long of light and air and grass,
The shyest flower is sweetest to uncover.

How poor I was: and yet no richer lover
Discovered joy so deep in earth and water;
And in the air that fades from blue to pearl,
And in a flower white-frocked like my small daughter.

Cold Morning Sky

Oh, morning fresh and clear as heavenly light,
Like warmth of love within the unwilling breast,
Sad to be so possessed,
Always the delicate shafts, piercing and bright,
Troubling my rest.

Neither tempestuous now, nor tormented
As when in fragrant, unforgotten air
Of the blood's April, all the world was spent
In passionate discontent,
In rapture and despair.

But like rich gold beat thin into a thread,
Metallic-firm and shadow-fine as thought,
So this new Eros rests his shining head
Upon a book much prized and seldom read,
Glad to be captured, shielded and untaught.

Then, under morning, everlasting morning,
Clear as new joy, cool with expectant breath,
The mystery takes blood, the arriving sun gives warning;
The soul within its sheath
Explains, endures, interprets all the bliss,
Once new and unexplained,
The lucid flower is named, the numbered kiss,
The pulse-beat numbered and reduced to this
And nothing is profaned.

But airy-light, oh, fragile, bitter-sweet,
A small bell rings and all enchantment's done
In smallest intervals of expanding dawn
Till quiet fills the eyes, lightens the feet,
Dissolves the wonder, all fulfilled, complete.

Dialogue

Voice from the old Hesperides
Suddenly rushing to my mind
Like quick rumor of the wind
Among the autumn-stricken trees.

"My beauty runs to seed
My rotting valor goes
To arm against your foes
In your growing need.

Neither man nor ghost am I
Who have come through deathless will

Neither time nor change can kill
To the chamber where you lie.

While I live in memory
Time will spare the scattered bones
They will rise from the grass, the stones
And the shattered tree.

From the pit and from the snare
From the poison in the blood
From the terror of dulled hair
From the phantom in the wood.

From the chilling of your veins
From the deathworm in your thought
From the falling of the rains
From the solstice and the drought."

Voice that I loved when young
Now that my earth grows old
Speaks with a stranger tongue
In the wind, in the cold.

Face from a banished tomb that peers
Pale through my window pane
What do you say again
After forgotten years?

"My long shed tears are dry
The dishonors of the tomb
Are locked in a little room
Dissolved in secrecy."

The Island

I sacrifice this island unto thee
And all whom I lov'd there, and who lov'd mee.
                                        —Donne

I give this island green in the green sea
To underseas of floating memory
Where all I loved and hated lie secure
In iceberg cold, jewel-frozen, diamond-pure
There once a boat with Christ's own banners set
Rose from a mist of cloudy-violet-jet
Against blue mountain-tops, and cold inhuman
Came from the shore the wails of ancient women.
Descend like that old saint, patrician, wise
Driving the evil serpents with your eyes
Descend like him to aboriginal dark
And on the heart of evil set your mark,
Green-growing trefoil of immortal love,
See the black ravens scattered, and your dove
Garlanded with the sacred mistletoe
While the druid voices rise in anger, grow
Until the Latin music drowns the sound.

The sacred maidens dance nor touch the ground
So light, so vibrant, so ethereally
Rose-petals blown upon an angry sea
This land remembers, must forever hold
Music of wind-wet silver, and that sense
Of low, subdued, and secret violence.
And the shawled women praying, the bare feet
The green-eyed children, ruddy, ragged, fleet
The emerald waters sheeted in green glass
The hills of shaded violet, green-black grass
And the faint odor of dissolving snow
When first the young buds on the blackthorn blow.

This aboriginal landscape, primitive
Drives me far westward where I cannot live.
Oh, to the warmer, gentler, happier South
My soul draws closer, to relieve its drought
Not this lost isle, this West that leans to North
Can I survive? I send this message forth
To you, the bravest of survivors. Look and lean
From your high tower of vision, all is green.
This land is in your blood, you will prefer
To be this chill's, this mist's, interpreter.

Voyage

Meet me where sky and air
Shine upon antique marble, heaven-drowned land
Where golden apples fade on the sea strand
And where the stone-eyed gods, severe and tall,
Loom white and mythical.

Where all is poised forever glazed and clear
Above the drugged, unmoving atmosphere,
Where the skies sleep in some intenser blue
Than any known to you,
Time's motion is arrested, there we'll spend
Our love to some wise end.

Unmoor the dreaming ships that swan-like float
Diaphanous and rapt on heavy waters—
What starry music from unearthly throat
Rises from opaque waves, oh, what king's daughter?
What lovely trouble trembles in the sound
It sings of other ships that met disaster
Sailing to the lost isles of alabaster,
Or Cytherea, or Atlantis bound?

Unmoor the ghostly boats and let us go
To ports that no men know.
The map is in my heart and you shall see
Wide seas unknown to your geography,
Yet real, real, real as memories of our race,
That place unknown where our beginnings trace
All love, all beauty and all force
To its lost source.

[for Joanna]

The Émigrés

Oh, in a harsh suspicious time,
Suspicious time
Metallic angry, dark with war
Disturbing every heritage
That once made gold the poet's page
To dream of pastoral days when rage
Comes like a sickness through the door
Brings but confusion; reveries
That are disease.

Yet guard your sibyllic books, oh, love
Preserve for love
Old prophecies of happiness
When the lamb sleeps beside the lion
And when the panther's unleashed grace
In tamed delight shall roam a place
In some forgotten paradise
Fruitful and ripe and evergreen
Unserpented, serene.

Blind outcasts from an age of steel,
The steel-sharp age
Knowing retreat is sacrilege
And brings its painful penalties

Of loneliness, unease
Yet hides for fear behind old marble
The armless Venus, eyeless Jove
The Apollo of the shattered lyre
The little battered god of love

And sees no ancient solace near
Only the stealthy feet of fear
Unchanging through the changing year,
The death-changed year.

The Dream

In that rich burial ground where the levelled dead
Lie darkened in extinction, I have groped
Through solitudes like death, as hopeless, lonely.
The Gothic terror in suspended air,
The cemetery reached, I saw the flowers,
Live roots among the dead, blazing in dark
Red bloom on marble, purple on the tombs
Flushed in the light, like an expiring passion
No ghost, no shadow stirred.
The reassuring blood raced through my veins
Aware and deathless in the dead meadow
Stars, thick as clustered flowers, enriched the heavens.
And light as cold as ether tinted the tombs,
But at one tomb, the light fell down aslant:
"Approach, approach, and read, and know no more."

Through creeping moss I read my name, I know
My name obscured, my tomb the smallest there.
No cypress weeps, but the moon's steady eye
Brims on it with a studied, bright compassion,
Irrevocable as the spoken word, poignant as love.

Death Is the Serpent

This moment when the sun is ebbing slowly
And the hushed world retreats
I saw the danger approaching, the declining power
Of heat in my slow veins, the serpent coiled to spring
On the tired hour.

Death, the dark serpent, heavy-eyed and holy,
The expiring sunlight greets
God of the coming night in torment languishing
Till each decaying thing
Is purified in air, in rain, in fire.
It shall at last expire
When the young world shall send its new grass forth
And the new sun arise
To open the dead eyes.

Afternoon of a Doll

The mottled afternoon shall shade
Your face of wax, the pink, the ivory-colored
Beauty that charms with mediocrity
Our minds are pleased with easy comprehension.
Sit in your wicker chair, nor wind, nor shock
Nor the mind's darkness make your soul afraid;
Death in itself is but banality
When it breathes upon the fluffy, silver gold
Of your fine platinum-shining hair.
Let sunlight beat upon your exquisite frock.

When the toy drums go mute on tiny ears,
Reducing noise to its absurdity,
Let hobby horses, gay with wine-red saddles,
Prance for your motionless delight
And let the small boy, auburn-haired, green-eyed,

Display his reckless and equestrian pride
Before your daintiness, who sits and preens
In infinitesimal and waxen dreams.
Deride, deride the shrieking auto horns
That blare through city windows, traffic lights
Red, green, green, red through window screens,
And the harsh voices rising from the city
Without reverence, and without pity.

Girl and Scarecrow

With wide cool eyes she gazes on mankind
And through its eyes her inward sweetness looks
Mirror-reflected. All dark thoughts refined
Purified as in a thousand mountain brooks.

Her own face seems mankind's, young, kind, dew-clear
Transformed by deepsea music it has heard
Her voice strained sweet and cold; in atmosphere
Like after rain, warm colors washed and blurred.

She knows the world is joy's and she can bless
Each day to come with a rich miracle
And draw time to her in a swift caress
While music flows from some fresh-rising well.

But time has ceased to breathe upon her glass
And when she looks she sees another face
Rise from behind the mirrored wilderness
With frantic arms outstretched for an embrace.

Face of a scarecrow sorrow-worn and sick
Emaciated, pale, a death's head way
Of smiling. Limbs loose, eyes of a lunatic.
Grosser than dust, a little less than clay.

The Runaway

Silent and stealthy days that hour by hour
Spring up unnoticed as a flower
In summer grass; and like a breath, a light, a feather
Make my world's weather.
I wished to weave a garland, deep and rare,
To wear upon my hair,
Or a long chain, intricate, strong and fine
To sound through stillness and to shine,
To bind the intangible days that so efface
Themselves with me, and run so dull a pace.
O they have run! they have gone! nor have they set
Their seal of vast regret
Upon that wide and echoing door
That, opening, opens, shuts and sounds no more.
How to pursue Life's Runaway? Let go
The innumerable sands that through my fingers flow?
Forgo the moons and waters of the mind:
Today is all that you shall find.

. . .

From "The Listening Landscape"

1941

. . .

The White Dress

Imperceptively the world became haunted by her white dress.
Walking in forest or garden, he would start to see
Her flying form; sudden, swift, brief as a caress
The flash of her white dress against a darkening tree.

And with forced unconcern, withheld desire, and pain
He beheld her at night and when sleepless in his bed
Her light footfalls seemed loud as cymbals; deep as his disdain,
Her whiteness entered his heart, flowed through from feet to head.

Or it was her face at a window, her swift knock at the door,
Then she appeared in her white dress, her face as white as her gown;
Like snow in midsummer she came and left the rich day poor;
And the sun chilled and grew higher, remote, and the moon slipped down.

So the years passed; more fierce in pursuit her image grew;
She became the dream abjured, the ill uncured, the deed undone,
The life one never lived, the answer one never knew
Till the white shadow swayed the moon, stayed the expiring sun,

Until at his life's end, the shadow of the white face, the white dress
Became his inmost thought, his private wound, the word unspoken,
All that he cherished in failure, all that had failed his success;
She became the crystal orb, half-seen, untouched, unbroken.

There on his death bed, kneeling at the bed's foot, he trembling saw,
The image of the Mother-Goddess, enormous, archaic, cruel,

Overpowering the universe, creating her own inexorable law,
Molded of stone, but her fire and ice flooded the room like a pool.

And she was the shadow in the white dress, no longer slight and flying,
But solid as death. Her cold, firm, downward look,
Brought close to the dissolving mind the marvellous act of dying,
And on her lap, the clasped, closed, iron book.

Quiet Countries: The World of Hans Christian Andersen

Now only when the skies are washed, rain-cleared
(A porcelain world so long the child-endeared),
Does his loose, rambling figure stride sungilt grass,
Watching woodcutter, clown, king, goosegirl pass,
Creating a world's dawn in every clime,
An unsealed fountain and a peacock time
Shedding its brilliant colors on the air
Unfolding worlds of marvel hidden there.

The transfigured swan whose meaning twice refined
Floats on the opening lake of the child's mind
And the tin soldier takes the unending field
And yields to life the sky-reflecting shield.
There where the early vision unbetrayed,
Shines in young eyes and is with love portrayed,
The stream of charm soon deepens every sense
Begins to guide our heart's experience.

Slowly the river of the swan flows down,
Runs through warm orchard land and trance'd town,
Stork-sheltering gables, flower-embanked canals,
The stream brims over, widening as it swells.
Hans Christian's town appears, blue misted hue,
Where all is myth, dream, revery come true.
From that light world of tears and smiling dreams
We draw our thoughts as from the living streams.

Through milky clouds, quiet countries we are led,
See on rich tables the fresh loaves of bread
Wild strawberries in green leaved baskets laid.
All that is born of dew and gleaming shade,
Fibred, webbed, fine, newgathered mushrooms lie,
That make one season gay, triumph and die
Things woven of dew, breathing the greenwood heat
That are surpassing rare, desired, and sweet.

To these quiet countries all birdsongs are blown,
World loved of children, for it is their own.
See how in heightened light, glad beauties gleam
On their soft cheeks like roseleaves dipped in cream.
And now the Master comes, gangling and tall,
Lighting the torches in the enchanted hall;
His words full of small meanings first, and then
They grow (each child grows) and are women and men
Deeper, darker, deep, the islanded Word expands
Into bright ocean, into greener lands.

Child in the Crystal

Through the world's low-water, the turn of the year,
He shines through crystal, rosy-tinctured, clear;
His soul is lit
In that white flame, by which the round earth spins.

All joy and sorrow, hope, fear, enmity,
All daysprings of desire run to a kindred sea,
But he enclosed in glass
Exudes his beauty like a field of flowers.

The heavens star-slit, expose that auroral sky
Where the desires long sleeping, wake and sigh;
The infant Time
Speaks of dewspangled lawns, of lutes turned to the wind's voice.

Seen only as a face reflected in crisped and turning air,
His lustre enriches the summer, his small hand dimpled bare,
Touches the sybilline leaves
And in the wind, the prophetic books are scattered.

Of his voice, breath, essence, grace, an image grows,
Ripens like yellow light, expands into rising suns,
Angel of harmony
In whose small heart the eternal clockbeat ticks.

Counting the unborn hours, the opening regions of joy,
Fire-flash on fine webbed clouds, the imprisoned boy
Sparkles—till bells
Of delight, timbred with fire, accent the declining day.

Forest of Arden

Expectant, hushed the air. Sounds heard when the earthly ear
Unlocks to immortal sound. Here the unsleeping dead
Sent early to the dark seek out the sun
Walk invisibly in the living solitude.
Whitely the spirit smoulders through the bone
When skeleton clean and clear the bodies shine
And move with the linear purity of a frieze,
They part the airy trees. Invisible in the thick forest
Each one a multitude, each one alone.

What fruits does this land offer? What pleasures will it yield?
Fulfillment of what unobtainable joy? It is not barren,
But waits behind tangible worlds. Here the spent minds restore
The final meaning to the relinquished shore
Recall the scattered lives that inward, downward flow
Time shrinks, long grasses deepen and grow.

And wait, watch the consuming solitude that lifts
The body down and seaward buoys up the spirit, flies

To dream-drenched forests, shows you their wonders.
Here is the jewel-capped snake whose lust never dies,
Ambition, power, and pride, the desire of the eye and the mind,
Insatiate, unquiet, it moves; its secret anger wakes
The mysterious powers of the dead that pierce the living.

Interview in Midsummer

Deep were the woods and the birdsong
Was oversweet and overlong;
The river tumbled through stoneways,
The long ferns dipped in dew would gaze
At my reflection in the pool
Unquiet, abstracted, never cool
Whitening like them through widening glass
At what was coming and would pass
Between us and the genial sun
When the midsummer day was done.

Yet happy, happy, was the time
Of liquid golden air, the clime
Of ease and joy and wildflower grace,
Of singing trees and cobweb lace,
Daisy and fragile buttercup,
Gay, slight-stemmed heads held lightly up,
Bowing and dancing in the wood,
Sprites of the whispering solitude.

Now riding slowly through the gleam,
The stranger came—face seen in dream,
Under the slim and sweeping willow,
Or troubled sleep on the hard pillow,
With no surprise, with no alarms,
I knew that face; oft in my arms
Have held that graceful form, that head,
Nightlong on the destined bed.

His face and eyes and form behold,
That at the appointed station told,
The hereditary enemy
That veiled but known identity,
In the long sought for stranger, trace
(Even while locked in his embrace)
Shadows of warning and distress
In the warm smile, the light caress.

Then ancient sadness dark and still
Put out the brightness, long and chill
Sweet, sharp, and cold, the nightfires leap
From smouldering chasms old and steep
As if a fiery spirit hid,
Its bright eyes through a coffin lid
Blazing through steel and wood and stone,
And made their restless vision known.

The wild air thickened as I stood,
Trembling in the silenced wood,
The voice, form, eyes encompassed me
In sadness and intensity,
Before I felt his pallor flow
Into my veins, I named my foe
Nor did love lessen, nor the pain
Nor did I wish my life again.

And then the sun in quick strong gold
Poured down a light, so spry and bold
The spellbound river danced to sea,
The trance-imprisoned clouds shone free
Candour and joy and innocence,
Where all was violence and suspense
And memory, passion, conflict, lost
While sun and shadow, danced, knit, intercrossed.

The Séance

When will that voice come? Drawn from the air in that drab room,
The plain table, the yellow curtains slowly fading,
The bare stone floor,
Wind on the roof mocking the spirit's gloom,
A knocking at the mind's door.

O but that Voice arrived marvellous, young and gay
Death shaking the young spirit loose
From the corruptions of the grave
Had shed his soul on ever-widening day,
The luminous body rising from decay.

Now by the wound still marked on the quieted breast,
Agony, defeat, despair, each grief defied, checked,
Tell how the iron gates sound,
In that vast netherworld whose meaning's unexpressed
Grew candid, clear, direct.

Century after century of silence, war upon war
Since in the autumn on a noonstruck hill
Your brief and lovely years were told
And the slow oncoming sea
Drew in that scarlet and that gold.

"Say that the early dead mature, in the dark, the mold,
Grow ripe in ungathered powers, sleep in rich chastity,
(In that fruitful bed). Whose children never born
Haunt us in visions of eternity
Perceptive, delicate, and cold.

"Say that shortlived Beauty is a stronger force than death
Complex among the simple elements,
It long survives the fiercer, brutal dead,
Charm, grace, and sweetness draw an enduring breath,
Their smiling spell, sky-drawn, tranced, overhead."

These things the exquisite lost Voice once said to me,
Till the plain table glowed with sun, the curtains shone
With faith's fine texture of light,
The floors rain-washed in cool serenity,
Reflecting spirit eyes, withdrawn and bright.

Snowstorm in January

Calm is the season, cold and clear the air,
Deep cold by which the dreaming blood is stung,
Heightened to clarity and made aware
Of the dark skeleton of trees and houses stripped of sun,
Grass chilled by snowcalm air, and gray quiet everywhere.

In other lands in mirrors of ice, I saw
The ancient winter of the soul, and magnified
Hectic, ablaze, and glittering without flaw
That burning town from which all warmth had died
While ivory pure and linear black and white
Beneath an everlasting winter night
Shone every January branch, each icy spellbound thing
Calm, calm, as on a summer evening.

Clear whiteness brighter than the sun's warm bronze,
Swan feathered snow! chained landscape taut and light
All richness covered now and grown austere,
As the chilled earth unfolds to deepening sight,
Then warning, premonition, and restraint,
Acceptance, resignation, and the fleet
Naked footfalls of joy, forever flying,
Till the dawn break and frozen fears depart,
Endure the silences, closed winter heart.

The Casket of Pandora

When for a long time I contemplate this box
Carved so cunningly by the hand of a god
Glittering with withheld treasure

I take no delight in my eye's light, the body's pleasure.

How many times awake, or in sleep, a voice
Through the open window, from the earth or the shore,
Says "This thing, this thing, you must not explore."

The shade of evil falls on the pure grass;
It shoots up from my life's root, its face
Troubling the emptiness of clear water.

And somewhere in my dream, the sound of pain and slaughter.

Then waking in my room, the casket gleams;
The maiden pallor of the morning light
Pierces my heart with an unnatural night

For in my world it is always morning;
The dew refreshes the mind, the early flowers
Hint of a delicate spring, foretell a green summer.

Now always at my door, the step of a newcomer

Whose face I never see though I open the door,
Though I look through sun-struck windows,
Though I peer through the enchanted dawn.

Then I touch the casket's lid, jewel-bright as dew on the lawn,

Locked, locked as a scent in a closed flower's heart,
O, to open the glittering box, to shut my ears
To the small voice that seems to sound from a tree.

Through my window the tree takes shape, has a face I cannot see,

High, marvelous tree! half-sun, half, wine-dark.
I feel the murmur run through your sap like blood
Eager for the deed to be done, wild to be understood!

Head of Medusa

How long she waited for her executioner!
She who froze life to stone, whose hissing hair
Once grew as waved and flowing as the sea,
Ash-damp and dreadful now. The fabulous mystery, the shame,
Forever in that cave where man nor beast came

Came and returned to life; so great the curse
Of the invulnerable enemy whose eyes immerse
Medusa's soul in this foul universe,
Turns her warm body passionate, fleshed with fire,
Into this loathsome thing no men desire

Cast in the final loneliness she must lie
Knowing that all who look on her will die
(The savage sorrow frozen in her sigh)
Even as she meets the look of fear and hate.
Their blood dries and their flesh must expiate.

But now her Perseus comes, foe or deliverer?
Bringing the welcome end. For whom her serpents stir,
Brute force and animal terror, the soul's tormentor
Subside; low-water calm, slow, unperceptively
Comes he who sets her free.

And now the end nears. Through steelpoint warm blood
Shall flow in purification. Her world made clean and good,
Through pain the Immortal's hatred is withstood.

Even now in the gold shield
One faces her, his life-blood uncongealed,

Prepares for the quick stroke that sets her free
From the cold terror in all eyes that see.
Even now the slayer's hand displays the mystery
That once vainglorious and guilty head,
Emptied of all its sorrow and its dread!

Background with Harpsichord

Domenico Scarlatti (1685–1757)

At the harpsichord I see him cool-fingered, fleet,
Drawing the notes that float, light, liquid, clear,
And live beyond the touch, while round and sweet
The dying modulations strike the ear.

Scarlatti, whose precise, pure talent drew
The greater Bach as dawn prefigures day
Into an altered world you never knew,
I heard you sigh who sighing seemed to say:

"What are my melodies drawn into air
But tones that seek to please not guide the heart?
The urbane pastoral no longer known, found fair.
By worlds whose needs demand a sterner part."

No, no, for we are women still and men,
Know weakness in our childhood; pensive, aspiring, fond
Our youth is always and will be again,
While life renews itself in the beyond.

Still let these small notes of perfection break
Upon the troubled heart, the arrogant mind.
Even on the war-stained landscape they awake
The tranquil joy we seek and rarely find.

The Familiar

I loved a shadow long ago,
Long, long ago in childhood he
Walked close beside me airily,
His spirit still entreating me.

Whether my foe or friend was he
My soul in his strong spell was bound.
He drew dead voices from the ground,
The menace of maturity
Gleamed from his body like a wound.

Low voices warning without sound
Spoke of a danger drawing near.
I heard the voices, felt the fear
But in my shadow's music drowned
Only the dry grass seemed to stir.

No living voices lovelier
Than his who sang close at my side
Of worlds whose light our planets hide,
Rich worlds, he their ambassador
Revealed to me, to none beside.

"And will you leave me now?" he cried,
His eyes of beauty in their force
Troubling my blood's warm, natural source,
Melting my bones, lowering my pride
Forgetting how his voices lied.

Deceiving, fatal, poisoning me
Exiled from heaven and from home,
Destroying root and flower and tree,
Release, relent and set me free
From *terra lemnia* where I roam
Release, relent and let me be.

Release, relent and set me free
Then, when my days are done, I'll know
The sound of human feet on snow,
Release what you have left of me
To hear the cock of daylight crow.

See seasonal blossoms ripen, grow
Into the warm and vibrant air,
Feel sun through stiffened limbs and hair.
Salvage my days that scattered flow
Like phantoms on a moving stair.

The Interpreter of Silence

*And thou shalt be brought down, and shalt
speak out of the ground, and thy speech shall be
low out of the dust, and thy voice shall be as
of one that hath a familiar spirit out of the
ground, and thy speech shall whisper out of the
dust.*
—Isaiah 29:4

Isolation is populous, it has many voices
Shrill sounding, fern-fine; silence has many faces,
Thin-eared, has sensitive long hands, is delicate in choices.

It prays on the deserted lawn, the suburban summer,
Waits for the feet that must come, that never come,
The familiar tread of the awaited guest, the startling newcomer.

The pink and white magnolia tree is stirred
By rumors of one who comes to pluck her blossoms;
It questions the breeze, it shakes at the sound of a bird.

Meanwhile the watching windows facing streams,
Reflect the nervous air, thin glass on watery grass
They dream of the sun's power, his strength, his life compelling beams.

The sensitive children play fresh voiced as fountains
Their arms are full of flowers; they are always singing,
It is not for them that we wait; they fly as birds to the mountains.

Why do you wait? for whom do you pray? whose hidden voice divining
The Prince of the Host of the Air, mailed angel, mighty cherubim
Who comes as a thief in the night, star-sprayed water-streaming.

From the stone towers of Assyria, mounted on the sun's horse,
He shall speak the word that shall splinter the night,
He will set the bushes afire, divert the swift stream from its course.

The interpreter of silence, the consoler of patient pain,
Who arrives in unguarded quiet, dismounts, knocks at the gate,
For whom the magnolia listens, for whom the children sing and wait.

Silence and the Wayfarer

Now the sirens have a still more fatal weapon
than their song, namely their silence. And
though admittedly such a thing has never
happened it is still conceivable that someone
might have escaped from their singing, but
from their silence certainly never.
                —Franz Kafka

Enter the siren quiet, wave upon glittering wave,
From land's end to sky's height, the age unloosens
Its emissaries of death, bland grace on mobile waters,
Veiling destruction and the suicide's madness;
Now a child's world unfolds, petal on petal, leaf on leaf,
The fatal island smiling in the sea,
Vainglorious arches, towering obelisks,
Enormities and splendors seen in sleep,
And sweet lips singing the unbearable psalm,
Always unheard! the opening floods of song heavy and calm.

From that deep sea where Love's own mother rose
We turn away, now is our voyage ended,
Now is our ship embarked on homeward waters,
We have survived; spirits of the darkening waves,
Escaped the treacherous waters, jagged rock, the ocean precipice,
Where sit the voiceless sirens whitely gleaming,
Green-gilt hair, eyes of sea-green, blue-veined bodies, foam tinted,
Thrilling the wayfarer with certain danger.

The rush of choral rivers silenced and strong,
Is in our hearts forever. Inarticulate as the still sirens
Our speech shall be. We have not heard but *felt*
That hooded song, that gaping melody;
Not in long lost Ithaca shall the wayfarer rest
And watch the hearth's fat flame,
For the old siren-silence stirs the blood,
Forever moving with the troubled waves,
Imagination rises from the sea.

The Listening Landscape

Now the children are asleep
Night uncharts its diagram;
In the suburbs women weep,
And no hero comforts them.
Now the prophecies come true
That the cards and stars foretold
And the reckoning is due,
And the sun is lunar-cold.

Innocence and Justice wait
At the mouldy, opening door
Carved with fabled beasts, and Hate
Takes its station at the gate.
Presenting arms the sentinels
March to guard the sleeping land,

Mustered from their several hells
The mute, rebellious angels stand.

Evening stupor, slyly mad,
Corrodes the heart, engenders truth,
Exploits the nightmares you have had,
Reveals the errors of your youth.
You shall see the pointed finger
Mark you out from other men
And the pin-prick wound will linger
Never to be healed again.

Hide no secrets now, for all
All must be revealed and told
As the bells of judgment call
Melancholy, stern and cold.
Hearing them the children wake,
At the sound Love's eyes grow dark,
In each flower a sleeping snake
And the arrows pierce the mark.

All, all shall learn the treasure hid
In your secluded rooms, shall know
The name, the hour, and what you did
And where your private gardens blow.
And the Recording Judge marks down
The buried fear, the secret sigh,
Exposed to all the prying town
What saps your strength, what drains your warm blood dry!

The Unsepulchred, 1914–1918

On scattered battlefields they lie
A generation's promise, withering
The manly hearts, the vigorous minds
Pierced by war's deadliest sting.

And you whom we lament, Owen and Hulme,
Impetuous Brezska, Isaac Rosenberg,
The young unnumbered; dying mute, unheard
In untried powers, new generations rise,

Trample, and thrust, destroy; corruptions creep
From ruined worlds you died to save,
The fine eyes close on a sardonic dream
Spent in the nightmare of the grave.

The wild horses of revenge are loose
Dyed in your blood's lost red;
The girls you loved grow old,
Their sons bleed as you've bled.

Children with alien eyes
Feel you as shadows frightening and low
While to new regiments the buried anger spreads
Frustrations; hatreds grow.

Hatred has known its seed
And sown new death on ancient battlefields,
The young blood festers in the grass,
The mildew rots the mock-heroic shields.

Now are the cities dark that once were bright,
Emptied of women's voices, children's song;
While overhead the death from heaven is feared
And underground, the shelters terror-deep.

Still under country skies, deep grass, soft flower,
The white topped mountain gleams; the water falls;
The ivory-breasted sea
From earth to heaven calls.

But unnamed dread takes shape, destroys the world.
Each wasted generation lies

In guilt upon our minds, unconscious blight,
Another darkening of the skies.

[for Bryher]

Leaves from the Book of Dorothy Wordsworth

FIRST MEMORIES

The garden, the rose hedges, the crisp-cut privet,
And the sound of the river,
The feudal twilight over pastoral Europe,
Low on the opening sky;
A threatening hand, large, occult and invisible,
Unrest in the young blood,
The century's decorous eyes lit from within,
All spoke to your infant eyes in the century's evening,
In the dawn's hush
From instinctive fountains, from clear source of rivers.

Light on the moorland pools;
Summer in a full rush of daisies golden-eyed,
The bluebell's delicate cup
Spirited, waving in the wind, the intense blue petals
Purpling, deepening in the sunny season,
And through the long deep grass the young feet wavering, learning
Wide fields where thrush and bullfinch sing.
The lark's clear note,
Piercing and high above the unopening graves,
Voices of unspoken desires, voices of the resentful dead,
Unbodied voices stir the red nasturtiums,
Now is your life-map clear, marked is the soul's journey,
The earliest road on which we always travel,
Footprints of the invisible.

THE SOUL'S JOURNEY

Hand in hand with the small brother
In orphaned love
Wandering through summer fields watching the gypsies roam
Through moorland wind;
Each day a renewal of wonder, each day the growing
Of a checked passion, the warm blood rising and flowing,
Fluttering of fire on the hearth, disturbing as the clock's tick
Silence, depression, and loneliness encircling quiet and quick.

Look through closed windows then!
And see the golden wedge of daffodils
Near stones green-damp with moss,
Dark crows in fluid flight
Taking dim shapes like swiftly rushing water,
Shadowy, flooding damp stones,
The slowly darkening green.
O from that living flood
"Teach me to draw tranquility into my uneasy blood."

"And the boys were always good, I was always a termagant,"
One day the sources of her life failed her:
She saw the white fringe of the sea running through black hills
Plowing into white skies
And knew the world had changed.
But over midland lakes summer and delicate green.

Here in the earth's heart summer and peace secure
The small brother's form grown godlike and mature,
All rivers running to the kindred sea,
Even so the uneasy blood finds presages, omens of worlds to be
In thee, O earth, mirror of ungained serenity.

Remembering the old woman on the farthest Hebrides
Sea-voices haunting barren strands
Wind-tortured islands straining part

Sky-line from watery land
The broken music of the human heart
Wild with an unnamed bliss
"Surely there is a great promise for virgins in heaven."

FOOTPRINTS OF THE INVISIBLE

Land-birds, sea-birds wheeling across invisible skies
Across the impassive sea;
The brother's form overpowering as the sea
Shepherds silhouetted in sun, the young lambs white and tender
Sea voices on the land, land voices heard from the sea
The raindrops fine as the pearls on a fine lady's ring
Fall soft, unmurmuring
On flowers, earth's happiest garlands marking the seasons,
Wild marjoram, early crocus, jonquils and daffodils
Colors of earth, sky, mood
Translated color of the blood,
Late flowers: the winter-cherry, the china aster, late flowering tea roses
All by the great time-shifter planted, ordered,
Duly noted by the thinking eyes in the mind's casket hoarded.

PROCESSION OF THE SEASONS

The music of the rain, the garlands of grass
The evening star sheds down hypnotic powers
Of sounds, rain music, wild wind harmonies
Into an ever green morass
Where the soul petrifies and feelings freeze
Till drop by drop the dew stirs sleeping ground
Falls trembling on the soul like water on a wound.

COLERIDGE

Not as when I saw him at the last,
The grotesque, dropsical body worn with sick desires,
The broken will, the eyes

Burning with fitful fires,
But as in youth we met,—
How life flowed in with him,
Danger and power and delight,
The torment of delight between us both,
Depth, strength and sweetness re-creating life
A splendor on bare boughs, a revelation
Shaping the world in majesty and might.

Thought like a flash of light across my path
Dashing with such rapidity, such spiritual fire,
"I felt as if my life was snatched away:
Force from that darting form;
It moved my soul, it took my life away."

And now in later years the disease of the soul,
Deadness of feeling, slowness of perception.
Coleridge is thine—within me speech lies captive
Thought is forbidden to fly.

The lakes glitter in moonlight, the fields sleep
In tranced rivers of thought, birds in full concert singing;—
The last of youth is passing,
Courage of youth ebbs, falls away,
Silence alone will stay,
And through the departing passions dwindling, tame
In flickering light I see
Death mask of the adored enemy.

SHADOWS OF THE END

Outwardly all is calm, outwardly all restrained,
The stiff gesture, the heart's battlefield deserted
But the soul knows its ravages, counts its loss
Measures the weight and height of its secret cross.

Swept in by time, walled in by memory
The face expresses all; the sensual mind
Marks the forgotten body with its sign.
Anger is there, pain, grief, for all to see.

Outward quiet, the restrained gesture, nothing expressed,
But in the evenings sleepless nerves complain;
Pressing her brother's children to her breast
Her days are full but long nights bring unrest,
Again strange fears, and nameless voices, floating, forgotten airs
Sobbing, blasphemies and prayers.

The airy structure of the world departs,
Pinnacles, temples, arbors, golden towers
Melt in a cloud, frail as a young child's breath
Always arise again, always destroyed, undone,

So Coleridge looked, blinded by the great sun
Of Contemplation; daws and starlings pecked at him;
The eagle soul still splendid in his grief
And the remaining friends, our fears,
Pass over their abstracted hearts like a dull sea.
. . . . .
Breaking on the mind's tide with a slow chime,
The clock heard in her childhood beating slowly out of time.

BELLS OF VISION

Voices in the air and the long twilight to the soul appointed,
Dead among the living, living among the dead,
Each night death's waters enter my blood, rise in growing waves
From half-remembered graves
Remember dreams half-dreamed in infancy
"Dear, dark unfurnished head
Where is thy home, where thy tranquility?"

Marked for destruction now, O burning brand,
In the guilt pits of terror you will lie
Consumed by anger and futility.
Ever upon your eyes the monstrous dreams
Rise in obscene procession, powers and principalities
Whose rites have known no name in the known sun,
The heirs and lovers of the Evil One.
Voiceless, eyeless, terrors drained of blood
Powers beyond evil and good—
Venerable faces, prudent, warning, strict
Loud parrot voices from a burning tree—
Harsh cries, small moans,
Strange gutturals night and day
The obscure conflict wears your life away.

FINALE

Now man and beast and child and sheltering tree
And golden fern by gray-blue river bank
Melt in the tranquil air of evening.
The golden sun to evening waters came
Leaving a brilliant circlet of thin flame
On the long highway.

Love like a shining garland on your head
Lifts you now, Dorothy, and lights your way,
With all you failed to be, and all you did not say.
The fitful laughter and the brief cry fade
Into the gray and violet shade;
The morning star descends into the sea;
Rises to classic death, rigid tranquility.

Hear in the long procession rising high
The choral voices sounding from the sky.
Images of imperishable youth;
Holding in unvanquished hand the undying fire,
The welcoming torches, and the bridal choir

Sing of fulfilled desire,
Immortal among things corruptible!
Fresh flowers on the stripped skull;
Fragrant, forever bright
The shining circlet of light!

·   ·   ·

From "The Golden Mirror"

1944

•   •   •

The Castaways

No matter where they lived the same dream came
Of the invisible landlady whose voice
Quickened the air with a dark flame
The words they have always known, will always know
"You are unwanted! Go!"

And when they built a mansion and furnished it with art,
With love, with music, with the native flowers
It always happened, it was always the same,
The salon narrowed to a tomb,
Sometimes a servant's voice, or a voice from the chandelier,
"You have no business here."

And when they left for the remote island and became the idol
Of the indigenous tribe,
And were caressed, admired, and sheltered—then
Whose was the voice of blame?
That came when they assumed the garlands, the voice they knew
Saying "This is not for you, this is all untrue."

And in the parks on Sundays with nursemaids, lovers, flowers,
And the bands playing and the fountains rising
In silver liquid hours,
Whose was the enemy? who was to blame?
If suddenly the observant shadows start
And cry "Depart! Depart!"

Now they have chosen exile, they have found a secluded house
In the smallest city, in the stillest shelter,
And they speak only to the wounded, the hunted, the lame,
The long evenings, the longer mornings, the longest noons,
And they wait for the bell to ring, for the landlady to appear.
And are they wanted here?

Future in Miniature

Daydreaming child on the tenement roof
Who sat in the sullied sun and thought of joy,
The thin, the blue-veined hands in life's reproof,
Lay on the shabby lap, two wax, two useless flowers,

Lay patiently resigned to heavy-dropping hours
Or future vast beyond all hope and reason,
Desperate dreaming brought refreshing showers,
Fish from remote seas, fruit out of season,

Visions of winter roses, summer snows
Till the starved life grows ill with discontent—
Now the thin cheeks' unnatural pallor glows,
The feverish spirit flares, is quickly spent.

And the hard truth no illusion can refine—
Touched the unlearned eyes and sharpened them,
As the blue flowers on the celestial stem
Or faded clothing drying on a line

Unite in equal terror. Inner vision, outward gleam
Blur in cold heat upon her helpless hands,
Through soot-grey air she feels the future stream
On threatening streets, or lonely, hostile lands.

Woman at the Piano

Rippling in the ocean of that darkening room—
The music poured from the thin hands, widening, gathering
The floods of descending night, flying from the keys
The sound of memory, then the woman singing
Vibrant and full, the resonant echoes scattered
Into a stranger's language, into a foreign country.

The rococo clock on the mantel strikes out its chimes,
The dark wind sighing through the open windows
Sends in its signals, wishes, memories;
The withdrawn room grows immense with hallucination—
Clear woman's voice, long fingers whitely straying
Over the speaking keys, do you hear the answer?
Will the male voice answer? stirring through the walls
Behind the rustling curtains, in the declining light,
Another voice still silent seems to tremble.

Patience is all. Unloved, unlovable, lonely,
It sits on the neglected sofa, watches the fingers
Draw out the difficult music, hears the finale
Shatter the torpor of the dying room.
Now the trees through open windows aspire and flame,
Now there are footsteps, echoes, reveries;—
Now two voices sound in the room where only one
Wove intricate sweetness from the simple keys,
Two voices ring in the dawn, the morning enters.

Variations on a Theme by George Herbert

After so many deaths to breathe again,
To see the clouded windows open, brighten
With recovered sight. To see the blackness whiten
And fountained love gush from the arid plain.

"After so many deaths to live and write."
Thou subtle God of Visions who has led
My footsteps to this room, this hour, this night
That I might testify my resurrection.

Now song pours from a thousand instruments
And my new-opened eyes drink in the sound,
The seeing ear, the thinking, speaking heart,
Refreshed again after long banishments.

Praise for the dark that taught me love of light!
Praise for the ill that made me long for health,
Praise for the death that taught me all life is,
I praise the mortal wound that made me His!

The Old House

If but this reticent house would speak,
If but its formal dignity
Would open to the sky, its trance forsake,
If but the dawn would break, the shadows flee,
If in the ancient churchyard miles away
The tombs discover what was locked from day.

I walked the ancient house and sought a key
To open chambers where the dead had slept,
A faded portrait guarded memory,
And a wide staircase its close secret kept;—
And none above, below, no living men
Knew how to breathe that name again.

But sweet the unnamed Presence everywhere,
Reflections of that bright admired hair
Stream in the buried grass,
From overseas the fatal footsteps pass,

Sad, drawn across the treacherous wastes toward home;—
No more, no more, you roam.

But point your spell to the old house again
Where the three aged sisters congregate,
The Mistresses of Fate
Who walked the house, who paced the narrow street,
Through storm, through rain, through wind, through heat
Reservedly and gravely, pensively,
In the rich dress of an old century.
Who shed the final tears, who spun the fatal thread,
And all your unlived years inherited.

The Winter Rose

The winter rose I saw
On its thin stem of glass
Shattered upon the grass,
Slain by its secret flaw

Red tarnished into grey
Recalls its world anew,
How its bright spectre flew
From endless blue to blue
Into an azure day.

Still, still, its beauties lost,
Despised, unloved, forsaken
Can charm the dawn to waken
In an arrested frost.

But ashen hues suffice
(The long ignominy
Of inert memory)
Who stemmed from that great tree,
That flamed with fire and ice.

Where is that look of fire?
Form, fragrance, height, and hue
The flame's expiring blue,
Life's thin electric wire?

Midsummer eyes will dress
Your elegaic dream,
Caught in a moving stream
Of unborn loveliness,
The dead will rise and bless!

Epitaph for a Careless Beauty

How carelessly you wore your beauty!
Lightly as if 'twere cloth of air,
Too heavy for your soul to wear,
As if to deny your gifts a duty,
Alas, for now you sigh
To see your graces fly.

That white hand, that rosy tinge,
Upon the cheek's deep pallor caught—
Mounting and rising with your thought,
The dark hair's soft fringe
That on the high wide forehead lay—
And the eyes burning brown
That no heart could disown.

As after a dull gala-day
A rich indifferent girl
Throws down each moon-clear pearl
That on small ear tips lay,
Precious and gay,
Or an exquisite gown,
Thrown idly down.

So careless of your gifts you walked—
Lost in a vision's gleam
Or pale abstraction, ghostly dream,
While close behind Love's shadow stalked
Until with his last sigh,
You turned and saw him die.

In mid-way of your path you heard that cry—
And from his quiver of gold,
The last arrow, stinging hot and cold,
Unsealed your blood no longer frozen dry
Kindling the fires unsated,
Passionate, unabated.

The fires that chill your life, torment the mind,
Even the enrapt vision gone,
The Platonic fury it has fed upon
Hears love's sigh on every wind,
Looks in an endless urn that now discloses
Embers of joy, ashes of roses.

Dream Message

From broken sleep I rose, from dream as clear as truth,
Eager dreamwalker, I paced the dawn,
Saw the eternal postman walking by
In the enlarged mist that lies between sleep and waking,
Thrust my quick hand out for the thick letter,
Saw how that hand was shaking.

I walked in the courtyard, stood in a rippling lawn
That in uncertain light grew wider, wide—
Expanded, brightened in the dreaming sky.
There under dawnlight, seal after seal breaking,
I read the letter expecting words made flesh, made blood, made bread,
Words without mystery or dread,

But the ink was blurred, the words broken, obscured the message—
What did you say, dear friend? from what wells of sleep
Have the half-tones, the broken signals come?
Through shattered sleep I fall, down the sheer passage
Of thwarted life, the strained distorted years,
Angry, unfalling tears.

The letter drops from my hand. I see it shine and blow
In the first wind of morning crumble away
As if consumed by an internal flame,
Fierce as unspoken love, the tantalus words calling
As they have so many years, days, hours
Through city streets, through country flowers.

For a Child

Lost as that ring that on my finger sparkles,
Hidden from all until my hand is lifted,
So in a quiet light in light adoring
My heart is lifted,

Runs steady, warm, and quick with love of you,
Of the wide eyes, the opening mind, the graceful
Body that radiates light, in light returning
Day after day.

This hidden love, my strength, my silent fountain,
My source of energy, my spirit's jewel,
My listless days, my heavy thoughts refining
Into a rush of sun.

I arm for your sake, I cast off sadness, slough
Fears and inactions, threatening doubts and shadows,
Wearing you on my heart as Rupert's cavaliers wore
Lace over armour.

"All Is Well with the Child"

I saw you arise from your bed, I saw your door open
Into a room flowering and falling with flame,

Into that room you came.

I feared for you, I followed, I called your name:

And you walked unharmed through the fire three times in flame,
You plunged and scorched to the soul returned, renewed, unharmed,
And the flames thinned to ashes, fell in a waiting urn.

Pallid with dying light I saw the day return.

No mind could penetrate, no eye discern
In what perpetual lives and deaths you breathed and drew
Strength for another life, another death.
That all was well with you the awakening sunlight knew.

Then without anguish, indifferent, calm, and reconciled
I heard the voice in my heart: "All is well with the child,"
And lilacs sprang into bloom, it was spring, the air was mild,

And again the voice said: "All is well with the child."

The Blue Flower

How fervent-strong and heaven-deep the blue
Of a slight tall-stemmed flower that I drew
From her obscure secluded family.
For often did I half-observing see

The fiery, delicate hue shadowing lighter grass
Hidden against sharp rock, or dank crevasse,

Where few wayfarers pass,
And felt the neglected blue shine deeply, passively;—

Though small the brief uncherished flower that shone
On the harsh stonescape of this exhausted land,
Beauty's supernal air was shown
Tender and helpless as a child's hand,
And though unknown, unnamed, to my regret
I thought you sister to the violet
And drew you to that gazing world of light
Where the proud rose sheds beauty full and bright.

Too frail, too soft, too small, to be uprooted,
Too blue, too heaven-serene to face the glare
Of summer's gaze on petals lightly fluted,
Ah, better to have left you on the rock
Between the stream-moist grass where thick clouds flock,
Left you unplucked, forgotten, spared you where
Your scattered sisters lift their skyblue stare.
And slender, burning under no man's eye
Fade in the pale indifference of the sky.

Luna and Leopardi

At the world's turning, at the hour of darkness,
When through the open window slowly rising
The full and beautiful moon poured lucid light
(O subdued gentleness of dying things)
Streaming into the room, shaking with nervous quiet
On empty tables and through trembling curtains
On the dark, steady floor.

Antique image of Luna, pale, full-breasted virgin,
Your glittering shafts of gold pierced every window
Entered the heart where dark and longing mingled,
Entered the avid brain and left its wound,

Invisible, never bleeding, dulled with pain,
Asking the unspoken question never answered,
"Are you alive? How long have you been buried?"

A dog barked. The voice of Daphne sighing in the laurel
Answered his harsher with a softer tone,
And both implored the night in love and pity,
"Divine satellite of day, pale-shining Luna,
Ambassadress-companion of the Sun,
Assure us of your favor and compassion."

And she rising from her bed of clouds—
Languid and ailing in the waning world,
Spoke in her voiceless speech through moving stars;—
"Never shall you have a cry of love from me,
Nor from the generative earth, nor from the Sun
The understanding-uncompassionate.

The majesty of human suffering
I can revere who burning like the Sun
Chill like man's age or girl's voice in the tree,
Or change from form to form like the Great Mother
Who mirrors in each form the changing world,
The fire, the water, and the blood.

I, Luna, too, reflect the shifting world,
The virgin image of the indifferent Mother,
I, too, can nourish life, am served by eunuchs,
The soldier virile in his death, the panting steed,
The firm-eyed serpent and the gentle deer,
The imagined phoenix and the unicorn."

Then in the darkness in the thoughtful evening,
All questions died into a various query,
"Are you alive?" or "Can you face the Sun?"
Know that the hour grows late, the reprieve uncoming,
The guards are waiting at the threshold of the Sun.

Can you endure the silence of that silver bed?
Enormous in the caverns of the Moon,
Far, far, from all the pleasures of the Sun.

The Affliction of William Cowper

Nature revives again, but a soul once
slain lives no more.
                    —Cowper

The fear was always there. It lurked in early love,
It hid behind my mother's hidden eyes,
Riverfalls, mountains, glaciers of the soul
Rose upward in hysteria, and from pole to pole
I saw the morning fly. I saw the darkness rise,
And Satan descend in the form of a dove.

A soul once slain lives no more
But there were nymphs in the grotto, goldfish in the bowl,
The frivolous Duchess danced in the cotillion,
All powder, lace, and feathers, but I saw
The rent in the girdle, the beauty turned to baldness
And madness arrive a conqueror on a great stallion.

Hares in the garden, pigeons cooing tenderness,
But dead is the immortal soul that courted You,
Dreadful, implacable, God, Judge, Lover, Tormentor.
We are the marked of Heaven who dare not speak
The singled-for-damnation, the unique;—
The vain, sad, hours descend, from skies of gentler blue.

Soft skies of shifting azure drowned in delicate light,
I saw Your blazing Centre thick with night,
I hear my doom announced in a quiet voice,
And know of no appeal. There is no hope, no choice.
I retire to the small house in a village street,
Hear from the harpsichord a tinkling sharp, clear, sweet.

Or a woman's voice in tender pathos singing,
A rabbit's furtive run outdoors, a silken garment's flounce,
Or, best of all, see grass in freshness springing
Out of the kindly earth, the warm maternal breast,
(Our perilous Mother at her loveliest)
And hear the Father's voice demand, command, denounce.

Secure, innocent, peaceful, but the thistle sorrow
Will rise some unexpected day in some idyllic hour;
It will speak through a bird, it will breathe through a flower,
The feared, enchanting face may come in sleep
And draw me through blue forests twisted, tangled, deep
Into some vast obsession called "Tomorrow."

And Ann may sing, and Mary play, and the fire burn
And frost and wind outside make shelter sweet—
But a gulf opens and I try to name the sin
That drew me slowly to the steep ravine,
That flung me into the abyss. I strive to name the turn,
The subtle flaw, that made destruction fleet.

Solitary, cut off from hope, the stricken deer
Pierced by the wrath of God. It faints in solitude,
Sees lustre of the Heavens washed and clear,
Made sacred by young light, made human by a tear,
The human tear that reaches Heaven's Lord
And is as poignant as a prayer, as wounding as a sword.

In that vast gulf between my God and me
No prayer can fly, no sword can pierce the heart
That is cast out by Him, and sinks alone apart,
Some invisible guard pushes the poison from our hand,
The knife pressed to the heart breaks—
A warning bell its iron music shakes.

The rope falls from the gibbet, and condemned to breath,
An agony of steep eternity;—

Forever in the interior dark, I sit and write,
While the black Presence shades the simple land,
Tranquil I sit. I write the beautiful clear prose
From which my sorrow rises like a rose
Floats through the garden and the lonely heath

Till all my agony is purged of endless night,
Into that downfalling stream, a drowning laurel wreath.

The Golden Mirror

And you are startled when your reflected face
In the full midstream of your sight becomes
A mirror streaming back your secret light,
All private meaning brought to public day,
Your thoughts reflected in your eyes and brow,
Your fate runs in your blood.

The destined bloodstream purer, clearer, grown
And outward landscapes glow with inner gleams;—
Now difficult roads grow smooth, familiar,
The invisible presence stalking all your ways
Becomes a living voice, an attractive face,
And the swift seasons all unnoticed run
While you count out your days.

As in your bewildered, hard, and wistful Spring
The incredible hope was still to dream of Summer,
Or long for steel-fine cities gold with light—
Or brilliant window's glittering for your sake,
Or far green meadows known in revery.

The meadows are your own, sometimes the windows shone
In that high city no man owns forever;—
You stand in ripening fields, your task half-done,
The task half done, that is undone forever

And know yourself a stranger in that meadow
Which now seems almost yours.

Begin to heed your pulsebeats, count the hours,
Or recognize your own face in the mirror,
The private meaning in the familiar glass.
Live deeply to your end while life pours in like sun,
As Rilke pricking his hand upon a rose
Signed joyously with his infected blood,
The painful, personal death.

The Imperfect

These keys that draw their silent music out
As if in pain. O quiet harmonies!
Heard in the fine-drawn torments of the brain,
Not in the sky, nor in the wind-struck trees
These thoughts half-cleansed of their impurities
Still bear Apollo's seal, and the star's rout,
Leaves whisper meanings to the initiate;—
And though not fully beautiful or great,
The unfinished glories speak to the devout.

Graceful, formal, slow, they call the dance,
The seeking spirit moves the creative spring
Of true delight. What hidden voice murmuring
Recalled some stately saraband or pavanne
Of Italy or France? Some ballet danced to Lully's strains?
When queens and princes moved to starry measure,
In dignity profounder than all pleasure
Pensive and gliding as the moving swan.

Or like Chopin whose sickroom insight lent
A nervous sweetness to a vulgar age,
Delicate, refined, the dying fingers spent
In fervid and bright jewel-edged melodies,

He sat in the exciting rooms as on a stage
And watched the thrilling warm-eyed dancers fly
Through his deep trance through each half-shut eye,
Saw also how his spirit's brilliant force
Moved with the dancers in that living frieze,
The hectic-flushed, the countless-countesses
Who forgot ennui under candlelight.

· · ·

From "Selected Poems"

1954

●   ●   ●

May Morning: Hudson Pastoral

The morning of the world, the western afternoon,
Cold on the American green, eternal youth renewing
Even as on Hudson's stream—
Cole, Inness, Durand, fixed the legend and gleam,

Made mythical that beauty, freshness, wildness
Pierced by a light, thin-bright as gold-spun hair,
The genius of the place in ecstacy
Rose naked in a young antiquity.

And saw with eyes pure-chill as the May breeze,
The young America that ripened there
Classic and gothic shadows interlaced,
Green-dappled, dancing streams embraced.

Dear sky-rapt stream, O green-reflecting river,
Wait, wait, for one whose music long delayed,
Your foam-green branches seek—
Seek, find their flowering tongues and speak,

Speak in the white lilac's breath, the narcissi's spear,
Purple-fanged iris, pink-flushed apple spray,
Each flower-frail world that flows
To reach the season of the rose.

Upon the white veranda one will stand,
Until light's revelation grows so fine

It seems time's silver-silenced shoes
Are worn by Bryant's or by Freneau's muse

And the evasive river silver-silent, gliding,
Gathers its green-garnered, legend-growing treasury,
Opens its watery arms and singing, sliding, runs
To deeper gold, and copper-coinèd suns.

[For Ruth and John Stephan]

A Friend's Song

Soon to reach you where you are—
Faraway—O dear to me,
Far away and very far
From silence and hostility
Rise the cities where you roam
Far away and far from home.

Stretching out my spirit hand,
I can touch you where you lie
In the much-contested land
Where the wounded heroes sigh,
Far away the lullaby
Of the sullen beach and strand,
Far away and far from me.

Neither rock, nor reef, nor snow,
Neither death nor calumny
Neither the wild stress and flow
Of storm and tempest, wind and woe
Of the ship-wreck ridden sea
Can turn, or change, or take from me
Longing, love, and constancy.

The Mirrored Room

Into the mirrored room, her eyes glazed and remote,
She walked silk shod upon gold,
Winter silver, the summer gold
Death shivered in her fur coat.

All things she touched grew clean and clear,
The china clock, the gilded chair
Assumed a rigid, classic air,
The golden haze grew high, austere.

The curtains hung mute, motionless,
Through noontide windows the sun dial
Brimmed thick with dark. A little while
All things seemed dim but her red silk streaming dress!

Through doors of glass and chill we heard
That dreamy, gentle, and unhuman
Voice that was not of mortal woman
Nor voice of angel, nor of bird.

We followed her through waves of frost
And saw her multiple figures pass
Floating through walls of ice and glass,
The guardians of the trapped, tamed, lost.

"Why, why, chill lady, fur wrapped, virgin cold,
Does your red gown shed color and flame
Upon a fear that has no name,
Why turn to silver all our gold?

And why the silent, sidelong look,
The glance that burns the world away,
Cold as the streams of a mountain brook
Yet vivid as the eye of day?"

Siren Music

Like an immense white flower in a dream,
You rise from a vast sleep,
Forever floating on a coral sea,
The sirens weep—
But now these glassy tears commemorate
All that denied by fate
Sweeps softly on the shunned, the outcast's door
And pleads for one joy more.

I saw the coral islands rise at last
And the great flower unclose,
The beauty and the fragrance no man knows,
Visions that leave aghast
The shrunken heart, still longing for the sea,
And all its secret, green hostility.
            [In Memoriam T. C. W.—1912–1950]

Song of the Forsaken Lilac Tree

Year after year the moon
Struck the illimitable silences and now
It glitters on the snow;
Soon it will freeze the little lilac tree
That longs to bloom and grow.

The fresh season tuned its leaves,
Heart-shaped, purple-laden
Where now the immense silence grieves.
Some lonely maiden
Gathers the unseen sheaves,

The graceful blossoms and their piercing scent,
The beauty burning fine and innocent,
Fainting beneath the moon,

And the air trembles and the solitude
Sinks in this lunar swoon.

I shall not see my lilacs clear the air
In bursting fountains of spring's essence glowing
Upon the deserted stair
In that neglected house and garden where
Memory retains its fixed and guilty stare.

Flower and tree and scent through time sway.
The moon will carry the guilt away—
It was not meant to stay.

The Twisted Tree

Too brief the sunlight when it smote
Our summer-haunted life! but caught
The dark tree's slowly brightening thought,
Saw fruit of fire and snow
Upon the topmost bough
And felt with love that gaze of fire,
The body sick with lost desire
And heard the sad, once lovely note
Through choirs of change and evening float
Beneath the twisted tree,
The twisted spellbound tree.

I heard the bird of morning sing,
Rise phoenix-like and shimmering
In sudden holiday.
We let our forgotten bodies air
In streams of daybreak freshening, new
And saw the sky's recurrent blue
Through dark and cold, through fire and dew
The bird sang everywhere

Beneath the trembling tree,
The shivering storm-wracked tree.

Then in our bones and in our blood
The black autumnal flood
Ran clear in sleeping veins and ran
Through pure wild sunburst, and the air
Revealed its sun-struck beauty—joy!
Joy! Joy! reborn leaped into flower!
Once more Joy blessed the living hour
Lit up the twisted tree,
The nine-time twisted tree of death.

·　·　·

From "Terraces of Light"

1960

. . .

Girl in a Library

The libraries consumed by passionate eyes—

Warm, eager eyes consumed by the dry print
Years lost in avid reading till the world,
Its landscapes and its figures and its thought
Stretched to a room's span.

The rushing years
Greet you with scorn who lift your frightened glance
To where the young Spring crescent of the moon
Seeks Venus her companion in the heavens—
Rain-pure and sure, they spill their beauty down
Till the closed suburbs gain a wilder air.

And now the whirling library seems cold,
Drained of its life's blood, now the eyes
Gather delights no more to feed the mind—
Only the young flesh mourns, the sensuous mind
Pines for the storm, dreams of the sun's embrace.

Whose was that restless shadow on the wall?

The Snowy Woods

The woods are lapped in snow,
The levelled buried plain;
They once were mine I know.

Familiar slept the grain
Planted so long ago.

Through hostile oceans now
I passed and once again
In my mild evening glow
Once more I see the rain
Flowing from ice and snow.

Land of my childhood where
I never flowered or grew.
The slow ebb in my blood
Quickens to answer you.

Skies where my first thoughts knew
Life's magic view
And the first lyric rains
Against cold window panes

I mount your aerial stair
Reaching into no-where.

The white snow on my hair.

Variation on a Polish Folk Song

Joy! Joy! Joy! that on my quiet day
In the dull house where never a sound
Echoed and entered, where I sat forever waiting,
The long, gray shadow crossed my way;
I saw the renowned greyhound
Speeding across dry fields, across my floor,
So clean, sand-sprinkled, poor.

An ardent beast, half-tamed, hesitating,
I thought him till his eyes shot flame;

They seemed to call me to the illimitable lands,
Into the very far,
Till I forgot my world, my life, my name.
And then I heard the unearthly wail of a horn
Sound from the world of the unborn,

And a red-ringed falling star.
And galloping across my field on a black horse,
A lone, fiery Hussar,
Who smiled and looked at me
While the great greyhound licked my hands.

Gently he waits, his mute eyes speak to me
(Unintelligible and irresistible the call!)
Of the great, patient animal
Who spoke in the Hussar's eyes,
Who drove his madman's course,
Flies skyward with my soul on his black horse
Toward some great, groaning sea,
Who sends his greyhound emissary!

Day after day I lie and talk to him,
Helpless on my sick-bed,
In the mute language of the seraphim,
And by unbearable longing led
My closing eyes are humbly questioning.
Tell me, O lean, fierce creature, gently bred
Of your Master, the Lord of the Dead,
Who brings such learning to the poor unread,
Whom the falling constellations bring,
And the tempest's whirling wing,
Who takes the Hussar's form,
And rides in angry beauty through the storm!

Four Ghosts

Four ghosts now walk the Russian forests, girls
Made of fine mists, rain-showers, snow-empearled
Angels of the snowy wastes, wraiths of a dead star,
The murdered daughters of the czar.

Each with a blood-stained ruby on her breast.
The frozen forest knows them, and the lilac-tinted snow:
The Siberian depths receive them and unblest
In flying death, the imperial eagles freeze—
Trapped in foreordained mortality. The East and West
Tire of their dying cries, but strange unrest
Through historic skies, echo the fatal melodies.

The blood-stained jewels on each breast will burn
Till the last eagle fails and the last shriek,
Till the soul's winter melts, and resurrection blows
Toward that spiked peak where no compassion flows.

Late Arrival

Love came so late, so late
Slow-sliding, silent, slow,
Deep and insatiate
And drowned in sullen sleep.

Then like the amoretti
Italian frescoes show
So frivolously, so lightly
Thin-pointing arrows glow

Into my heart, my blood
Slight, light, and gay;
I could not if I would
Withstand their play.

The soundless Word I heard,
The Love whose blazing dart
Pierces the midnight heart.
The buried landscape stirred

All in a maytime green,
Singular, fresh, and clear,
A water-wavering scene
In April atmosphere.

Love's Herald then I saw
For whom the spirit yearns,
For whom the round world turns,
The Guardian of the law,

Who fixes in the soul
Magnanimous control
And Justice without flaw
For whom the seasons roll.

Elegy and Nocturne for Lora Baxter

Within the waxen lotus gleams the jewel.
Stretch out your hand lost friend and touch it where
Illumination shadows your white hand, bright hair
That like water in a pale stream
Flows where the brilliant ice-peaks burn and gleam.

This was your sun-filled life, it leaped, it glowed
A jewel in the lotus heart, light fell in diamond clusters,
The mountain peaks loomed high, bright passions fever high
Poured a white light at noon like the moon's silver thrown
on a blue river's ever changing lusters.

Lovely were the hours—
Happy, happy were the birds that sang above the short-lived flowers

Green-breasted, scarlet-winged, and emerald, tawny, dappled
Never again such color and songs happy, upspringing free.
Do they sing still in your vast sea?

Song

Life with her weary eyes,
Smiles, and lifts high her horn
Of plenty and surprise,
Not so where I was born

In the dark streets of fear,
In the damp houses where greed
Grew sharper every year
Through hunger and through need.

Lest the harsh atmosphere
Corrode, defeat, destroy
I built a world too clear,
Too luminous for joy.

Unnatural day on night
I built—tall tower on tower,
Bright on supernal light
Transfixed the too-bright flower.

But see how it has grown!
The cold dream melts, the frost
Dissolves,—the dream has sown
A harvest never lost.

Blood runs into the veins,
The wild hair in the wind
Waves in the natural rains;
The harsh world and unkind

Smiles, and its eye grown mild
Surveys this nothingness
Like an indifferent child
Too sleepy to undress.

Song for a Season

In the quick fresh season
How often have you lain
Your head in the clouds, and the rain
Refreshing the dry reason—
And the vanishing earth
Dropped down like a pearl,
Pear-flushed without stain,
So fair life's form, so bright its pace,
Rich with its quick and slain.

Never will the berry drop
From its red cluster,
Never will the peach tree bow
Into your famous grave
And make a death-wreath for your skull,
A garland for your brow.

It is forever now;
The song will never be heard.
Who will trap the flying bird?
And your hands so fine and clever?
And those sad, witty eyes
Who has borne them away
In the kingdom of forever
Will they return and stay?

Voices in Air

Do you remember? (one said) and they rose from their long sleep
The mock tournament, the feast, and the smile in my eyes
When I pinned the trophy on your breast,
I cannot remember the rest.
Do you remember? (he said) that it was winter then
And the horses were waiting, eager to depart
But the long banquet hall was lit with a thousand lights
And your cloudy silver gown was sprayed
With starlight, moonlight
And we danced the hours away.

Never to meet again we parted:
The trumpets blew the centuries away
And now on clouds of fire, of fiery snow we sing
Of what the hastening seasons sometimes bring.

I remember the hours (she said) when January turned to May—
Fancy and wit and ease, made holiday
(He said) that glowing winter day,
Then into my saddle I sprung—

We were both destined to die young.

So in the clouds, so on the glimmering Hudson's air
They whispered and rose through naked cloudforms changing there,
Reliving one moment out of endless time,
Marking one season always in their rhyme.

Virgin with a Lamp

You have seen her in the procession, but alone,
Separate from the maiden group she comes
To the sinking altar, to the worn stone
Where the God once lingered, where in human days

He was known and loved, feared, honored, and obeyed
Over the lands, the mysterious lands, where his scepter swayed.

Cold and severe she stands—but I have heard
That when she walks the crumbling floors, wild light
Streams from her upheld lamp. Her life caught fire
And turned and flamed against the encroaching night
And she blessed the individual sky so soft and clear,
The warm domestic spell that trapped and drove her here
To the forgotten altar, to the great banished Lord
Whose prophecies came true but were not heard
Who sometimes speaks through the air with the voice of a bird
Magnificent, and tragic, and absurd.

The Question

Shall we have peace my soul
Or will eternal wars
Inflict their wounds, their scars?
It is not yours to know.

And does it matter when
Those eyes that follow me
Ghostlike and piercingly
See what they must not see?

And the locked treasury
That holds the hoard I hid—
This you spy out, forbid
Dear Lord of secrecy.

And the tears, the secret tears
Like summer frost, like winter flame.
Will you expose them all,
Dark tears that dimly fall
Like summer snow?

Great Lord of life, say No.
You will open every door,
Unlock each frozen river,
I shall wait no more.

From "The Fountains of Rome"

Flow, flow pure tears that from cold fountains run,
Fall on calm marble, tremble through the soul
And on the tender wings of the young angels rise,
The infant angels with their ancient eyes.

Have you not gardens now to rain upon
Glad tears? The patient heart your colophon?
Flow then upon each mouldering arch, each time-wrecked place,
Restore the words that wave and wind efface.

Surely some truth will leap, some buried God will shine,
Rise through some golden stream whose apathy
Time and the grave concealed. The fountain's race and rush
Unseals the trembling motion of the sea.

Hymn to Artemis, the Destroyer

Grey-eyed huntress in whose hair
The crescent moon unquiet lies,
Descending from your mountain stair
Spare the frightened hart—O spare
The warm heart that atrophies.

Under your moon-clouded gaze
The pearl-tipped, star-bright bow we see
Winging into sterile days,
Days devoid of hope and praise
Never fruitful, wide, or free.

Ah your blazing, stinging, arrow—
Chastity's too rigid flame!
The freezing dove, the starving sparrow
Flying, fall, and call your name.

Now from your cold mountain top
You descend—the harried deer
Spill their lifeblood, drop by drop:
All life's glowing motions stop
In an ecstacy of fear.

But the escaping soul that flies
Into warmer courts of air
Remembering your moon-shaded eyes
And your heaven-breathing hair
Ever for your presence sighs.

From a Winter Journal

Blow your cold trumpets too, Memory,
Mother of all the Muses answers you
And now her classic wreath and tunic drops
And naked as the morning sky she stands,
The golden trumpet in her snowveined hands.
Withdrawn Goddess, Nymph of the submerged fountain,
Mother of History, Queen of the fluid stream
Wherein the story of our race abides.
From your long, secret eyes, our vision speaks
And the fluid truth more intricate is seen
An eternal comment on life's changing scene—
The violet-frail, the delicate mystery
Of the great tides, the ever restless sea,
Rocks worn by ceaseless pressure, the buried city
Sunk under lava, burning all life away
Or swept through the long reaches of the sea
In a cold fury without pity,

Whether the marine world veils its plunder, or
The tight rose in the garden sways as it glows
Through the veiled Eyes where all compassion flows.

A Theme from Louise Labé
(c. 1524–1566)

Diana sleeping under the flowering apple tree
I saw in the green orchard. She arose
In wrath at my approach and said to me
"Nymph, nymph, where are your weapons for the chase,
These silver arrows my sworn maidens bear?
Now leave this singing green, this fertile valley.
Tomorrow all my girls go to the race.
The wild boars rage on the mountains, in the hollow
The panthers prowl, the sleek deer follow."

My weapons are all gone, O virgin queen,
My quiver broken, and my sandaled feet
Limp wounded. In a covert deep and green
A stranger seized my quiver and my arrows.
Beautiful he was and bold, and his touch harsh and hot;
He took my bow and aimed shot after shot
On my open heart. His indifferent laughter rings
Long after he has left. And the wound stings.

Terraces of Light

Where the drowsy landscape draws
Summer from a floating Eye,
Where the golden pathways lie
Expanding in gold rings of light
Quivering, tumbling bright on bright
Where the cup of dew is spent
In the glittering light of day,

Let us mount the steep ascent
To the castle, see the way!
Where the sleep-worn bastion towers—
Shimmering in a golden haze,
Hanging mountains twisted trees
Chill the running golden spray.

That ascent will bring us near
To the castle in the sky
Where the cloud foundations rise
On the brilliant atmosphere.
Further, further lies the prize
That man seeks before he dies
(Where the impelling hunger leads)
The visionary landscape pleads
The more than life-size roses sigh—
You have left the world behind,
Chilled the heart and drugged the mind
Seeking what you cannot find.

In the shadow of that Eye
Floating in an azure stream,
We have mounted dream on dream
To the terraces of light
Shed our lives away like leaves
That the first faint chill bereaves
Of volition—and lets fall
The season's measured festival,
Dropping in cold pools of thought,
All we treasured, all we sought,
And slowly, slowly, withering
The maimed, unfeeling, senses sting.

But through hanging waterfalls
Striking against greenest green,
Hardly hoping, scarcely seen
We have reached the castle walls

Entered through the mildewed halls
Seen the prostrate shadows flee
Forms of fear and phantasy
Cloaked in everlasting night
Fleeing in a blaze of light.

The Flowing of the River

Without remorse, without regret, without fear, without envy
I watch the flowing of the river as flows my life away.

Unperturbed by the bold wind rising, and the surf beating
On the storm-cleansed coast, refreshing the northern sky

With wind and waves and waters, with wild motion and joy
Never still, never fearful, joyful in deep dark plunging.

Beautiful the mornings, unveiled by the Dawn's white hand
Striking out time from the crystal clock of the hours.

The icebound streams now clear, forever released from winter,
Melt in the sun and shine, in a shower of stars and spray,

Tranquil and cool, active, wavering, winding, unweaving flow
Bright waves! dripping in sun, as a seabird unruffles its wings.

Whose are the drowning eyes plunged deep in deeper, deeper depth
Rising in circling gleams of light, mournful at nightfall?

Foretelling the season of silence, dreaming always of summer
Southward and ever southward, the days, the streams fly.

The Garden at Cliveden

Germantown, Pa., 1777

January not June. Then why the scent
Of wild heliotrope, of pale yellow roses,
Why ghostly music, and a measured dance
Of graceful shadows under the evening moon?
Then rise those phantoms whose vitality
Is greater than the living, whose quick blood stream
Is poured from the hectic moon. O thou Selene, Queen
Of the sleeping senses, do not scatter them,
Two lovers who now cross the garden, halt, embrace.

The centuries roll back, and yesterday
Is one with the flooded grass, one with the agile grace—
The quick retentive mind, that almost-caught
Genius from the compelling moon, subtle prophetic thought
From captive tides, from sharp air, from moving rivers, From each
 distinctive season's special dower
And one with the shy smile and delicate face,
One who loves more, one who loves less.
The season does not prosper. Selene does not bless
Her lovers, and her cold indifferent charm
Weaves the rough coils of hovering tragedy
With frustrate beauty of the sleeping moon.

Now locked (a moment) in each others arms
They move and then dissolve in history,
The wars, the eternal wars shall separate,
The dead must strew the garden, gunshot beat
Against the window panes, the bloodstains on the grass
Linger for centuries, lightly as autumn petals
Fall from a withering tree. So shall your loves pass—
One shall remember always—one forget.

And then how beautiful in memory
That winter scene, that arrested glow, when all

Was fulfilled in time, when all that ought to be
Took place in time, fulfillment of all passion
Under the moon, under the hostile moon
Beneath the living heavens, under the unfriendly stars.

Cascades and Fountains

Drawn from deep sleep, the dark, dim waters run,
Fountains of living waters night and day
That wash my life away.
Surely they gush from the dry rock, the thirsty sun,
Splendid and fertile, spraying the dead grass
With light as in a golden fastness.

Slow life, and slower change, muted, immutable,
Running like water quick and shallow, clear:
Dark year on hurrying year—
Beneath the glowing heaven, under the nimble heels
Of rushing worlds you keep
All that the sleepy and resentful dreamscape feels.

Fons rejuventutis,
healing flood—
The pure limbs of beauty enter you,
Energy fresh and brilliant, the reviving blood,
Warm eyes and springing hair
Meet in your flood, dissolve and are united there,
While the wild waters flood time's crumbling stair.

Toward the Atlantis of the soul you move:
Worlds flung underseas, an abyss closed and sealed,
Sources of life forgotten and revealed,
Foam alleluias rising from above
In watery peals of love,
Unlocking passions like a choral flood
That sings within the blood.

· · ·

From "Collected Poems"

1965

Spellbound

I looked and saw your life
In the shadow of your hair,
In the glory of your eyes—
Bells, bells, rang everywhere
On the storm-threatened air.

I looked and saw a light
In the shadow of your brow,
In the white power of your hand,
A whirl of wind and snow
Where golden angels stand
Gleaming against the night.

This was the moment when trees
Lifted their April arms
In a pale rush of green
Shading a moonlit scene
Casting their early charms
And their newborn dreams
In magic streams.

O then it was I saw
In the shadow of your hair,
In the dark power of your eyes,
The magnetic pull of the sea—
Earth's spellbound mystery
Strict in its changing law.

The World of the Salamanders

Slowly, and one by one, with few to see or hear
Above the chilling movement of the sea
The salamanders dripping gold appear.

Through trembling waters, over primal seas
They arise, and sing of fire, of fire-lit phantasies;
They summon marvels, legends, mysteries.

Then arise at their command from wind and wave
Divas, Peris, water-pale Undines
And mist-veiled weeping queens.

In wavering worlds of sleep, in the skull's cave they sing
A *gloria* in honor of their king.

Metaphysics of the Night

Our bones are scattered at the grave's mouth,
Our lives have fled before the certain tread
Of Time, she of the multiple disguises, she
Who in her many forms is never still.

How fresh and gay among the daffodils
In the April season by a gleaming river
We saw her first, quick, ardent, saffron-robed,
Free as the air, a dryad with sunstruck hair
Who moved in a green world, plucking white flowers.

White rose on fire! moss rose in a damp meadow
She seemed—firebright in a burning season
Green world on fire! air's freedom lightly shadowed
Immortality in modern dress appears
Disguised as Time, was Time, is Time itself
A gay green masquer in a crumbling world.

And now invisible among the stars
I hear her in the murmurs of the tide
Gliding through rainsoaked branches in the park
Hovering over banquets and the dance.

And violet-shadowed in the receding sea
And darkening mild Sunday afternoons
Her spectral image rises and restores
Solitude, certitude, and history.

Chorale for the Seasons

In the time of the scorpion we first came
To the forests floating in light, and the swaying shadows
Sun-dipped in moving gold,
Leaving despair behind, and a dark season,
The sting of malice, and the dangerous door,
O my bright scorpion!

Beautiful it was in the year of the Ram,
The wild flowers opening in love to the sun, the trees wavered
Warm in trembling air, fanning the seablue heaven:
There the children were always in white, and always singing
Oh my beautiful ones!
Time drew her curtain down, and veiled the scene.

It was best to live in the time of the running deer
Soft-eyed and wary, peering behind dark thickets
Or leaping through mist-wrapped mountains drinking in cool hollows,
O my doe with the fearful eyes!
It was your year of illusion, white is your shade on the mountain.

Slowly we wheeled into the cycle of the wild swans
When the rain flooded the earth, and the children departing
Spread their soft wings to the light, ascended to thundering heavens;
Left alone to the quiet of the moon, to the whirling waters,

Beautiful swans we salute you—
Flying into the unknown, landing in virgin skyscapes,
Exploring unborn stars.

Drifting, sauntering, see we have reached
The world of the water lilies

Only in dreams, when the spirit released, leaves her unwanted body
When the sun is obscured, and the night prepares
To unveil her starry shores—
In the white trance of the moon
O my white and golden lilies!

Now is the time when the demon that hides in the clouds,
The seawraiths that wail in the waters,
The storm spirits chained in the shaking woods,
Mix with the scorpions, mate with the wild swans,
Call to the golden Ram who grows fat in a prosperous meadow;
Timid the white doe drinks, returns to the shimmering pool
Where the young stars are drowning.
Drift like the stars, my soul,
My white and drifting lily.

Homage to Christina Rossetti

Silence of after-wars, when through the air
The high, leaf-dropping tree
Reflects the bright blue weather glowing there,
So still, so quiet your fame, diffused, yet nowhere:

Your dark Italian streams of English song
Poured such clear fountains down,
Delicate as a string of fine-matched pearls, as strong
As the fretted iron in the great Tuscan's crown:

And fresh as young-eyed seasons of the mind
When the heart bathes in sun and clouded streams grow clearer,
Or when the grave and golden autumns find
God's contemplative beauty closer, nearer.

Then best we praise you for your garlands' shading,
Death's feet and Love's, garlands of small, perfect roses,
Small roses few but perfect, never fading,
Brought from your secret heavens, startling our garden closes.

For you the Sacred Muse revealed her illumined way
And taught the single heart, devout and true,
How to praise God in fire-touched songs that pray,
Songs that Teresa heard, Siena's Catherine knew.

Then like a garland of pearls, or a stream of gold,
Or a great pillar of fire, or a small, wounded bird,
Your quiet gifts rang purest gold,
Rang finest silver, and were loved, were heard.

· · ·

From "The Hidden Waterfall"

1974

•　　　•　　　•

A Shakespearean Cycle

I. PROSPERO'S SOLILOQUY

Loud sounds the clock. I sit at home,
Free from tempests and mad storms.
Years have consumed me, passions worn.
My island sinks in sea and sand;
It drifts away—is No Man's Land.

Mystery shields me like a cloak,
Envelops me in my last age,
Robs me of my rich heritage—
The ever-living earth and air—
Strips me of longing and of care—
Drained of patience—hard as bone—
I now am free, am now alone.

In savage silence, spirit-guided,
When voices rose from harassed caves
I mastered men with alchemy;
I fettered wild beasts: through my law
They knelt, they feared, became my slaves.

Released from longing, sadness, shame,
From hatred festering in my breast,
I, who have known the worst and best,
Can gaze unmoved on all I see:
The fruitless triumph, or disgrace,
Injustice, and its haunted face.

The shipwreck on the madman's coast,
The ravaged wail, the spirit's sigh,
The sorrow of the long oppressed,
I shall remember till I die;
To have escaped much is my boast.

All evil done, in part undone—
My forfeit kingdom, lost and won,
I love at last, and can condone
All bitterness for a child's sake.
The quiet light that the stars make
Can bless at last, can now atone.
Voice sounding through the wounded air,
Set free of pride and vanity,
The stars at night will shelter me.
Shed is the anger, striving, pain.
I sail to exile once again.

II. PERDITA'S SONG

Cast, cast, adrift, disowned, disowning
You seek your father and your mother,
Too far from the safe tomb
You drift too long and drift forever
Under the willow-weeping grove,
Under the golden-gleaming orange tree,
Where shall you find your home?

The storm, in silent anguish rising,
Will strike your island's sleeping heart.
The rescuers seek but have not found you.
Soon the mastering tides will creep—
No voice shall bless, no eyes behold
Your glassy fountain's frozen wonder
Beneath whose silenced charm you lie.

Red is the moon, the cloud's unfolding
The lovely view no eye beholds;
Unshared the golden lamps of morning,
Unseen the silver bowl of night
Where the stars fall unloved, uncaring,
Where no heart bleeds, where no tears fall:
There let the great storm break.

III. CORDELIA'S SONG

Only the unloved know
The wild reach of the heart,
Vulnerable, sick with rage
That no word can assuage
So desperate is fate,
So inarticulate.

Did I not plead again
To the lost man in the rain,
Appealed to him in vain,
Forever tried to prove
That love was truly love,
Though wrung so clumsily
From the heart of pain?

Dearer than salt, than bread,
Your arrow in my breast
When life seemed weariest;
That love so strong, so deep
So difficult, unkind,
Fell like a star or flower
In caverns of the mind,
Blind, dark, and steep.

IV. MARIANA'S SONG

Wind on the aging house
Set in an emerald sea
Of summer-waving grass . . .
When will my deliverer pass
For whom I wait and wait
In mingled love and hate?
What will become of me?

There was a promise in the hall,
A messenger at the gate—
Some tokens came too late.
Soon, soon the forgotten stair
Sounds to a lost footfall.
Will he come to call?

Lonely is the house,
Within the moated grange
Nothing will ever change.
Time echoes everywhere
The clock chimes with an eerie
Languishing despair—
No one is ever there.
I sit and comb my hair.

The book falls from my hand
(An old tale is retold),
The flower dies in the glass,
It was thirsty and grew old:
It was undone
Without air, or sun.

Was that a knock on the door
Or a leaf falling?
Was it his voice I heard
Faltering, calling?

Morning is gone: the dark
Silence appalling.

Swimming in golden air,
In whispering, willow-waving summer grass,
Year after year the world springs up,
Fills with a clear green wine
My life's untasted cup,
Fantasies fester and thrive.
He will never arrive.

In that locked tower
Dust fell on my bright hair.
Sharp through the long corridors
I hear the creaking of unopened doors.
Was it the wind, or my fate
That made me wait,
Or bestial footsteps on the crumbling stair?

Iron-corroded sun
Seen through cracked window glass—
How fluid and free the shimmering twilight's gleam
In some unworldly dream of hill and stream
Where the wild deer unhurt, unhunted, run.

V. OPHELIA'S SONG

Eyes of despair, eyes of fire,
Watchful terror, warlike peace.
Quenched is the star of all desire:
It sings the song of my release.
I throw fresh garlands, white and red,
Into the devouring river bed.

The willows shiver as I pass.
I feel the trembling of the grass.

As the waves rise, and slide, and fall,
I sink through islands of dark water.

None shall remember, few recall
The early Spring's unhappy daughter
Whom amorous Death found loveliest.

No Prince can claim me, and no charm
Scoop from the waters my small flowers.
They drown in running wave and stream—
Pale Undines of some idle hours—
Lost in the willows' drowning gleam.

My floating, underwater bed,
My little garland, white and red,
Will know my name. The willows shed
Familiar shadows on my head.

As the flowers and the stream
Sink deep in elemental calm—
And the song, and the dream . . .

I shall not come to harm.

VI. MIRANDA'S SONG

To my island, late returning,
Since my life's meridian source
Shrinks in silence, silent music
Draws me hither.

Forms of beauty long departed,
Snake-green rivers lithely weaving,
All my flower-fine youth reviving,
And the dwindling moon
Kills the memory of rich cities
Worldly manners, charming strangers;

On this island let my morning
Soul its early music render.

How clear the springs! the forsaken island—
There the earliest winds caress me,
It is late, the jasmine blossoms
Fall like snow on fading tresses.

A Young Girl Singing

Through summer-sparkling days, when skies were bright,
In a white dress through a green stream of light
I walked in a naked world as if by candlelight
And heard through the wind-twisted blaze of the trees
That a new voice was crying in the sea-cold breeze;
As the grass, flowing like green water to my knees,
Ran in a rising stream of joy and praise
Of the sun-flooded, champagne-dizzy days,
Of the grass blowing and rising into a green-gold maze.
And the young voice that spoke through an invisible horn
Was the dry forest voice of the not-yet-born,
A voice like a fresh leaf from a green tree torn!

Water Lilies: A Nocturne

Once water lilies floated on this pool.
Now they are gone, only their phantoms sigh,
Only an old song to recall them by,
Only the memory of a world that flew
So fast and long ago that memories cool.

Gone are the lilies that I gazed upon
With the fond eyes of youth, the lilies white and fine,
To sadder, darker days I now resign

The weeping reeds that stand line upon line,
Grim relics of a world once fresh and new.

The midnight visions and the morning gleams
So rich with sunlight, starlight and bright streams.

Only the wild fowls of the marshes call,
Only the thin brown reeds hold the festival,
And I return, a shadow tamed and small,
Frail as the reeds, as mortal and as pale
Beneath the moon, beneath the moonlight's trail.

The Young Dancers

Now the reviving sea
Returns in summer waves
Where the young dancers fled
Whose image time engraves
(From some lost long ago)
Because of some gift, some grace,
That death could not deface.

Slow their approach, so slow,
We watch with anxious heart.
Nightfall they knew, and snow,
Have they forgotten their part?
It was their fate to play
A lifelong holiday.

Nightfall came soon, and snow
Descended on each head,
The known world turned to stone,
All the spectators gone,
In a forgotten place
Each played their role alone.

Restored to youth again
By the time-tide's force,
Life, like an untamed horse,
Runs the exciting shore.
Fine mind and exquisite face
Resume their cherished place,
They find their old allies.
Rare beauty never dies—
The dancers come once more.

In the keen air, in the sun's fire,
In an implacable desire
Renewed are the sea's advances
Resume, resume, the old dances,
And the song with the old refrain,
Renew our life again!

O Like a Young Tree

O like a young tree rooted near the water,
Foreseeing the fresh season, year by year
So let me stand.

Like the suave moss, grown thick on water's edge,
Warm under the tree's root, cooled by the driving wave
Let me endure.

Surprising, dewy bright as the wild strawberry
In leaves that form a basket green and fine
As ruddy and gay.

Or the June rose that springs up new and sweet,
Bride of the summer, child of summer rains
So fair adorned.

The lake-clear heart, fern-fresh, the brimming look
To face the dark, and the clear happy eyes
Of lake-drowned stars.

Let me ensnare for a leaf's span, for a flower's season
Joy's rosy, transient wing skied in the summer light
Warm and unshadowed.

Another Snowstorm

Do you remember, dear friend, the many snowstorms
We have endured? In a worn, too fragile house
How long could it last? We were trapped in cold,
We had seen so little of the sun,
So few of the glittering stars,
We never missed what we had always known
And now, another snow.

But the granary is full and the harvest sown.
Always through shaded windows beauty shone,
Despair played a music strange and clear,
We wrote it down;
Hope built a cheerful pathway for our feet.
We never knew defeat.

Now we are free of fear
In the white whirlwind of the year.
What we have feared came shamefaced and lame,
So worn, so tame,
We had forgotten its name.

But we knew that the Spring flowers would come again
Soon, ah, soon,
The small white flowers unhaunted by the moon,

Or the winter night,
Being so fragrant and bright.

Soon, soon the melting snow
And the air fresh and still,
Again the hyacinth and daffodil,
The little snowdrop growing in the rain—
We too begin again
Beyond pleasure or pain.

I Know an Island

I know an island, pale in the green sea
Where the Atlantic waves grow lost in mist,
Of delicate violet and pure amethyst,
Where the gray sea gulls rise monotonously.

Green, green the shoreline, rises cool and green,
The trees green, black, against a somber sky
Small purpling hills archaic and serene
Through lingering rains that fall deep, endlessly.

Step on this greenest, softest, dreamiest turf
To breathe the mystery this isle presents
And you shall hear the sound of violence
Subdued and hostile as the rising surf.

Saints, heroes, kings, and martyrs, waxed and waned
In this their ancient seat, gray-toned yet wild
In haggard beauty, subtle as a child,
How many times adored, subdued, profaned.

Lament of Catherine Howard, Fifth Queen of Henry VIII
(?–1542)

Happy in the sparkling green,
In the Maytime of my years,
Suddenly I saw the sky
Like crisp water, running clear,
Brightly, freshly, running clear.

For a feather in my cap,
For a ribbon in my hair,
For a jewel in my throat,
I had dared life's highest stair—
Life so young and debonair.

Then I met my aging king,
Rich and heavy, lustful, strong,
Easy ran my lute, each string
Wind and water, wave, prolong
Rich and rolling in the hall,
In the mirrored gallery
Rang the golden-timbred song.

To the violin and the lute
I have danced the Sun away,
Danced away my life and soul,
Danced old England fast away,
Danced away my new-found years,
Blood and violence and tears.

In the old king's trained bed,
Still my blood danced, youth and joy
Held a moment like a toy
Till the tainted blood grew cool
In the crimson damasked bed,
All my wanton moments fled.

Lust has dried the sparkling well
Of my dancing summertime;
Power, intrigue, dissolved the spell
'Twixt the bridegroom and the bride.
Weep for silly, pretty things,
Pleasure doomed to foul mishap
For a frock, a jewel, a ring,
For a flower on my cap.

Yet my true love doomed with me.
An iron house of constancy
Shields us both eternally,
Shields us from the fatal king,
Through this fate I have deserved
I have kept our parting vow,
"None shall ever say I swerved:
Time and the grave destroy and sever—
Constancy remains forever."

From "The Madness of Jean Jacques Rousseau"

(a poem in progress)

I

Aging, forsaken, passionate, and unloved,
Neighbors stone me. Silence blackens my door,
Knives always at my breast, but at my century's throat
I, too, can press a knife, inflict the healing wound;
I see the classic statues dripping blood.

As I appear, the harassed, murdered man,
Father of the castaways, lover of the damned,
The conqueror of the Alpine solitudes,
The walker on the abyss, the swan's interpreter,
When her dissolving image stains the world.

The east trumpet signals. On the lake
The brilliant glaciers melt! The orphaned children beckon,
All whom the earth disowns and God forgets
(And in the gilded salons tears are falling.)
I appear. I speak. I hold a book in my hand.

(1944)

II

Who reads my book reads all my life,
Who reads my countenance sees all my soul,
Come all who see, who feel, who read, who love,

Know that the heart is pure though the flesh fail,
Though the blood runs darkly to an impure sea.

I stand where Alpine torrents find their source,
Near lakes of fire that burn eternally,
Conspiring malice in its secret force
Destroys, torments me, casts me in that sea.

But born near Alpine mountains I can live
Lifted above my sins, I still can stand
A hated prophet in a hostile land
Through hatred and destruction far above
Alert and naked, eager to win love.

Why do averted eyes still follow me?
Deep at the center gleams the fatal flaw.

(1974)

The Invaders

A child runs in to play,
The child grown, now away,

The child that haunts my heart
By night, by day

Whose image fills the room,
Enveloping my days,
Engrossing all my ways,
Source of all prayers I raise.

The children grow, my flesh
Withdraws from the bright room,
The days, the days, unwind
My hopes, my fears, I find

Dream children dance and sway,
Enter my room and play
And when I leave they stay
By night or day.

Soon will the young fawn drink
Deep in the silver stream,
Soon will the morning sink
In a cold, pristine dream,

Soon will the children fly
Worlds upon worlds away—
But still they haunt my heart
By night, by day.

Bird and the Muse

The Muse that stirs my blood,
In unforeseen control
Takes form, becomes a bird
Blazing through realms of gold,

Leaves me so suddenly
I hardly know her gone,
In worlds remote from me
She flies through land and sea.

Although the unwilling soul
Shrinks from her brilliant flight
She must fulfill her role
Resume her mythic part
Enter the sleeping heart.

Write then although the walls
Close in with never a sound,
She chides, inspires, recalls
The rarely trodden ground.

Learn patiently to paint
The white face of your God
In the indifferent night
When all the senses faint.

She may again appear
Through heart and soul and mind
When your two eyes are blind
And days are dulled in fear.

Poor, lonely, her reward
The angelic note of praise
Your life must not record
Through all your days.

The Flying Victory
Lifts wounded wings, and sings,
Part Goddess and part bird,
I hear her passing sigh,
Her final whisperings.

Once in an Ancient Book

Once, in an ancient book,
Remembering what I read,
Lines scattered to the wind
Or buried in the sand,
Words quoted, widely spread,
Now lost to humankind
In a dry, dead land,

Still, still, some glory thrives,
Blooms and has many lives,
Through deepest memory
Retains strange influence—glows
In clear serenity
Through longing or repose.

It tells how beauty flows
In some obscure delight
Through pain, through failing sight,
Through subterranean streams
Of love, through the very soul
Longing to be made whole,
Or sees the dark made bright—
Sees also from a height
Some secret goal.

. . .

Translations

1960–1974

·   ·   ·

From the Italian of Claudio Achillini
(1614–1640)

Wars and of arms some sing, but I
Of other battles, wounds, and victories sing
The sound of men embattled and their cry;
No, not to these has my warm spirit turned,
I sing of Love, a warrior tall and fair
Who brought me all the sorrow that I knew
And all the beautiful, the good, the true;
Tell then, my heart, how you were vanquished,
Transfixed, and troubled by a lock of hair
And tell how many angry tears I shed
For a harsh look from two cold mocking eyes,
(More fatal in their killing glance than Mars'
Whose victories are as potent and as strong.)

'Tis *Amor, Amor* who has vanquished me,
He whom the seas extol, life's living rhythm praise,
He kills my heart but gives life to my song,
He shortens, but gives meaning to my days.

From the Italian of Cardinal Pietro Bembo
(1470–1547)

On the death of his brother

You, too, my brother in your hour of Spring
Left me too suddenly as if compelled

Lightly, and with a golden glittering—
As if your sparkling life was caught and held
In the large hand of time and dropped untimely where
Your eager world dissolves in the high air.
All that was wild and gay is now nowhere
And I reflected in your eyes shone too.
My mirrored shadow living in your grace,
Lived for a moment in your living face,
Now into silence, into death's disgrace,
Final injustice that gives none his due:
I too would leave my place, and follow you.

From the Italian of Michelangelo Buonarroti
(1475–1564)

My soul without a friend, without a guide,
Teaches me slowly, slowly, O too slow
To feel another's sorrow, and my pride,
Dear Lord of Fate! has made me shun Thy flag
Beneath whose sign, Your wounded legions go.

No triumph, Lord of Fate, but it is Thine—
Then lift my spirit, Lord, its slow decline
Has made my blood run low, my strivings lag
And tamed my talents grown too thin and fine.

Coward I am, who fears to see the light,
I hide within my art, while Time takes flight,
Too harsh to others, are my sins so light?

Mercy! I cry, O see my wound, my scar,
Too close I am to death, from God too far.

From the Italian of Lorenzo de'Medici

(1449–1492)

(Vida madonna sopra in fresco rio)

Beside a running brook my lady stands,
Green branches arched above her, and the skies
Reflected in the silver running tide.
Her face is seen as in an illumined book
Shadowed by evening winds when night demands
That all things end, when only night abides.
Forever stands her image now, it holds
That primal passionate look.

I saw in her young face, in her proud air
All time, all seasons run, the earth had veiled
All things, my youth, my sorrow, and my flame
My love, my longing, and my honored name.

Now always when the early spring revives
Memory, memory, lasting memory—
I feel this morning sweetness, pause and sway
Into a world of fountains, dancing spray
Where the inspiring vision still endures,
Nor like the stream shall ever float away.

From the Italian of Lorenzo de'Medici

(1449–1492)

Leave, Cytherea, your enchanted isle,
Remote, green-shaded is that Paradise:
Its crisp-cool waters, its rain-jeweled showers,
Its fountains rising to the ravished eyes . . .
Rest, white-limbed Goddess, while the magic waters
Multiply into fountains, sky-drawn springs,
Bathe in the rose-faint heavens while the clouds sail,

Move with the sun and hear the Sirens sing,
The fountains answer, and the streams prolong
That song of air, of water-wavering clouds.

Swan-guarded, close-locked world, O Cytherea,
Eternity at peace is mortal here,
Lured by the silver breath of purest song—
See how the love-lost seek your land and long
To claim the vistas of delight, they bring
The Sun-Seeker, he who leads them all,
Your laughing son, young Eros, winged and tall.

From the Italian of Vincenzo Monti
(1754–1823)

A coward thought has struck me: "See poor soul
How learning and the inner vision fail
And the red earth spins on, and night
Begins to drown, to dim the hopeful day—
The beloved faces smile but will not stay."

Then I replied: "And if my outer sight
Is lost, what harm is there? I see
A clearer, cleaner, a more dazzling light
That still embraces earth, explores the sky,
All things assume the heavenly shape; I see
The flying Beauty that has ravished me,
Fame and oblivion to Her are one,
Seen through Her eyes the pursuit of fame
Appears a childish thing. I woo the Sun."

From the Italian of Gaspara Stampa
(1523–1554)

Mesta e penitia dei miei gravi errori

With deep repentance for my wasted days,
Trivial thoughts and sensual desires
Squandering away my days, these few rare days
Of fugitive life to kindle dying fires.

To you, to you, my God in my despair
I turn at last and let your flaming snow
Upon my heart in sacred ardor glow—
Stretch forth your hand, for I am shipwrecked, float
In a black whirlpool, drifting, sinking, gone:
A ghost that rains and tempests beat upon,
I mourn my sins, I beg your aid once more,
Hopeful I turn, O weeping I deplore;
You who for all mankind did suffer loss
Desert me not, lean down from your high cross.

From the Italian of Gaspara Stampa
(1523–1554)

PORTRAIT OF HER LOVER

Ladies who ask me to portray my love,
The Lord who rules my world of whom I sing,
Picture him young, gay, elegant, erect,
Gay, witty, learned, high-bred, O everything
Youthful in years, mature in intellect,
Well-versed in men and books, skilled in the wars.

By what conjunction have our conflicting stars
Brought us together under Amor's wing
(Delightful God whose faith ebbs like the sea)

With him whose graces Jove rains from above,
Knowing perfection how it flies from me?

And ladies whom my portrait too must see
If honesty must guide a faltering tongue,
Tell of a face by passion marred and crossed,
By Death's strong image, haggard, tempest-tossed,
No longer worshipped and no longer young,
(The charming manner, the beguiling tongue)
Torn between longing from my love and grave.

A woman sick of silence and dry days
Whom neither tears, fame, eloquence can save,
Who dies forever in love's chilling gaze.

From the Italian of Torquato Tasso
(1544–1595)

White moon, star-strewn sky,
Night's mantle now is thrown
On you and the turning earth;
The darkening universe,
Seen through a crystal ring,
Gleams with a cloudy pallor.

Stars drop on the dark grass,
The empty silence dreams,
The wind withholds its voice
But trembles in the air.
The locked heart hears the sound:
Midnight now appears,
How cold the night, how cold!

Something is waiting here,
I hear it in the dark,
In the pale light of the moon

My sorrow will not pass.
A knife, moon-silver sharp,
Is thrust into my heart,
I feel but cannot bleed—

O life of my life!

Nine Variations on Themes from Petrarch
   (1304–1374)

I

Love, Love, cruel Love, long have you driven me
To follow the wild beast who drives you too
Where the dawn flowers in that exquisite blue
Of cloud and sealine on our summer shore—
The country that we lost and still adore—
From that country of hope, in fertile sunlight laid
We have brought back dead sea fruit, the sea anemone
And tarnished jewels, broken instruments
That made clear music once and may again
So beautiful your joy, so rare your pain:
I long for them again and long in vain
And now from shuttered skylights, still I see
How the young, the beautiful, still flock to thee.

II

With sleep, all evasion possible,
Naked and poor you go, my hidden spirit
To the deep fountains of old Helicon
Where the bright tree shoots up in limpid water
And where the bird of morning ever springs
On the light heart and spreads its glittering wings.

Deep in a grove of laurel weeping lies
The sacred Muse, Apollo's lyric daughter
Since Laura's soul descended to the skies—
Who led her dance, who learned her secret tongue
(Alas poor Muse! your summer days are long)
Since Laura sleeps—through empty days she goes
Where the still waves on the encroaching desert flows.

III

There, in the gay season, pale and cold
A young girl stands beneath a laurel tree
The sun had left her but her face and hair
Shone in the orchard where she used to dance
Under the tree, the sacred laurel tree,
Beneath the branches where gold apples hang.

So peaceful and serene her spirit seemed
That all things turned to flowering sprays of fire,
There, once where bright Apollo tuned his lyre
The notes of beauty, hope, fulfillment rang
Since in that world, the bird of morning sang.

And from green-haunted waves silent ran out
A waiting boat, guarded by Loves, I went
And floated toward some stranger element
Toward the lost continents, the ocean floor
And found myself alone on Memory's shore.

IV

I sing the hand that reached to enclose my fate,
Soft-skinned, snow-soft, soft-gloved so charmingly
That light gloved hand in springtime conquered me
A hand so small to enfold my destiny!

And I sing the eyes, the brow, the frown, the smile
That held all grace, desire, all innocence
Lulled by the falling waters of our death
As if the pristine world had caught its breath.

How far, how far away was the season of snow
And I prayed to Time, Time who allots to us
A moment when the senses sting and glow
A world of opening springs and wavering hope
And then reveals the scaffold and the sky
An abyss of threatening years, the hangman's rope,
And leaves us stranded on a perilous slope.

V

That was the day I saw the fatal rope
Coiled in a hand of ivory and of snow
Behind a curtain of dark, I hear my tired blood flow
But the white hand still beckons, beckons me.

Sweet is the bait it offers to the soul:
I follow the veiled dark, I bless that hand, and walk
Into a garden where all light has gone
And on invisible waters a lone swan
Praises the hand that dealt the sweetest wound
And then a golden bird sings overhead
In that deep silence where all song has fled
Extolling bells that rise from earth and toll
Praising the waters for their healing sound—
And still the two birds sing and will not fly
Through that pure darkness to the brooding sky.

VI

In a violet gown, in an azure stole
Star-glittering, carrying a crocus spear

The Goddess walks the mornings of the year
Following the Phoenix, the Arabian bird.

Following the bird whose flames of golden fire
Must forge the jewel for the Muse's throat,
The Muse I have most invoked, burning with heat, with
    blood,
Whose language I at last have understood.

Before I fail, the Goddess promised me
That I shall walk her grove, wear her attire
Woven of dewclear skies, heaven's softest hue
And drink the morning, taste infinity—
And see the golden bird of Paradise
Rise once and deathless to my waiting eyes!

VII

As I approach the last of all my days,
How small my world! How large its burden and pain!
And Love, whose charming face I wooed in vain,
Mocks me at last, eludes my yearning gaze.
Angry, embittered now, at your request
I'll sing no more. O love—your silver chain
I'll now unclasp—go forth now as you came,
A naked child exposed to wind and rain.

And in the dreamless world I'll lie at rest
Since love must die, then all things too must fall,
All earthly sorrow and resentment flies,
I see at last how worthless was the prize
I sought so long—so slight the sight, the touch—
We die for that which cannot matter much.

VIII

THE DOE AND THE LADY

In a glade of emerald where the shade
Glowed in the moongilt air of evening
A milk-white doe I saw, leaping through air and light
And brilliant as the waterfall her eyes,
Her topaz-tinted eyes.

Pale woman facing all your vanished beauty,
Where has it gone? why did this flying doe
Shed such a running trail of harmony,
A world of opening skies and glittering dew
On the sky-silvered blue?

In diamond letters on a collar of gold
Across the doe's white neck I saw inscribed
"Touch me at your peril, hinder not,
For my great sovereign the last king of kings,
The sky-descended, earth-engrossing emperor,
The Caesar of this world, the scourge of worlds to come,
Has left me free to roam the imagined world."

And now this doe roams through the flying air
And views through northmost outposts of despair
The green-gloomed, rock-rimmed sea.
And follows storms that fiercely urge her on
Into the rough-hewn ocean, where her gaze
Pierces the treacherous rockpools, where sea-flowers
Cast off their frozen powers.
Or where cool, cool, in chastity and dark
A seagirl's form is seen swift, flying, white
In deep insistent light
Casting white spells of healing and delight.

Then like a wind storm, fainter, lighter growing,
Swooning and drowning with the storm-bolt hour,
Her white breast like the moon, and ocean rises
To seaflow and to light.

Capture the doe, and draw it by surmise
To face the tempest dying in our eyes—
There in our captive eyes where all drowned beauty flows
The Heavenly Beast that never knows repose
Through emerald thickets flying,
Or where the Snow King's daughters
Rise on the angry waters.

IX

THE PILGRIM KNIGHT

And I followed the veiled form of the pilgrim knight
Because he was so beautiful, and because though doomed
All loved the ardors of that charming face
Who pitted passion and magnetic grace
Against those destroying powers that can efface
All that will make youth's journey a delight.

And following him through briars, through a savage wood
I saw him fade unconquered, and I stood
Watching his footsteps leave their trail of blood.

Nothing without travail and blood is wrought.
We saw that high intelligence and grace
Glitter through pain, that beauty dearly bought!
How strong the delicate chains that bound and caught
The iron Spirit that had led the dance
So frivolous, so touched with elegance!

Two Adaptations from Frederich Hölderlin
(1770–1843)

1

And you Diotima, who walk humbly among the living
Holy, obscure, and pure, a Goddess among barbarians
Men know you not—vainly you seek your kindred
Your sky-born equals.

Sages, and martyrs, virgins who have walked
In supernatural fields of living green
Paradise's closed arbor where the few,
The sacred few, pluck Paradisal flowers.

But from the dead, the great and tender dead
Who dropped from sensual time, and live
In aerial splendor with the darker Gods
Expect your tribute.

They wait to welcome you and my poor song
Lost in a whirlwind clime, you hardly hear.
It sings to drowsy ears, but names you now,
The name you bear in Heaven.

2

Too long we lived for work and wages, we
Have walked among the thorns, ignored the roses
But the day, the day is at hand so long in coming.
The cloud-filled world ignites, is full of light
The air is alive with birds. All the trees are in flower.
The white flowers kept for the last are grown
Though they seemed to droop, alive on the living tree
We can pluck them now. The rains have restored their beauty:
The violets that were crushed, revive again.

And the birds multi-colored, fall from azure clouds
And raise their choral music to the sun—
Darkness has fled while we slept. New skylines arise
Unknown to mortal eyes. It is forever summer.

It will always be light. We have forgotten the night
Time was, time is, and this one world remains
When the light of evening turns to purple and gold
In the storm, in the pure rain.

O ultimate beauty piercing heart and brain!
Enlighten us slow moving moon, and you O diamond
Bright falling stars, strong ever-moving sea
Glide on with us, beyond us, toward the light.

· · ·

Works by Marya Zaturenska

Index of Titles and First Lines

Works by Marya Zaturenska

Poetry

Threshold and Hearth, 1934
Cold Morning Sky, 1938
The Listening Landscape, 1941
The Golden Mirror, 1944
Selected Poems, 1954
Terraces of Light, 1960
Collected Poems, 1965
The Hidden Waterfall, 1974
New Selected Poems of Marya Zaturenska, edited by Robert Phillips, 2001

Prose

A History of American Poetry, 1900–1940, with Horace Gregory, 1946
Christina Rossetti: A Portrait with Background, 1949
The Diaries of Marya Zaturenska, 1938–1944, edited by Mary Beth Hinton, 2001

Anthologies and Editions

The Crystal Cabinet: An Introduction to Poetry, with Horace Gregory, 1963
Collected Poems of Sara Teasdale, 1966
Selected Poems of Christina Rossetti, 1970
The Silver Swan, with Horace Gregory, 1968
The Mentor Book of Religous Verse, with Horace Gregory, 1957
Afterword to *Love's Cross-Currents* by A. C. Swinburne, 1964

· · ·

Index of Titles and First Lines